GREAT QUESTIONS IN POLITICS SERIES

Is Voting for Young People?

MARTIN P. WATTENBERG
UNIVERSITY OF CALIFORNIA, IRVINE

PEARSON
Longman

New York • Boston • San Francisco
London • Toronto • Sydney • Tokyo • Singapore • Madrid
Mexico City • Munich • Paris • Cape Town • Hong Kong • Montreal

Vice President and Publisher:	Priscilla McGeehon
Editor in Chief:	Eric Stano
Series Editor:	George C. Edwards III, *Texas A & M University*
Editorial Assistant:	Donna Garnier
Marketing Manager:	Elizabeth Fogarty
Production Manager:	Savoula Amanatidis
Project Coordination and Text Design:	Elm Street Publishing Services, Inc.
Electronic Page Makeup:	Integra Software Services, Pvt. Ltd.
Cover Design Manager:	Nancy Danahy
Cover Designer:	Base Art Co.
Cover Image:	© Getty Images, Inc.
Manufacturing Manager:	Mary Fischer
Printer:	R.R. Donnelley and Sons Company— Harrisonburg
Cover Printer:	Phoenix Color Corporation

Library of Congress Cataloging-in-Publication Data
Wattenberg, Martin P., 1956–
   Is voting for young people? / Martin P. Wattenberg.
      p.   cm. — (Great questions in politics series)
   Includes bibliographical references and index.
   ISBN 0-321-43569-9 (pbk. : alk. paper)
   1. Young adults—Political activity.   2. Voting age.   3. Political participation.
   4. Political culture.   I. Title.   II. Series.
HQ799.P6W35 2007
324.90084'2—dc22

                                                                          2006003709

Please visit us at http://www.ablongman.com

ISBN 0-321-43569-9

1 2 3 4 5 6 7 8 9 10—DOH—09 08 07 06

For Mary

Contents

Series Preface

One of the most interesting—and disturbing—trends over the past 30 years has been the declining political participation of young adults throughout the world's advanced industrialized democracies. Moreover, there is a mutually reinforcing pattern that further widens the age bias in political participation. Many young people do not follow politics; therefore, they do not vote. Because relatively small percentages of young people vote, parties and politicians frequently neglect them. Naturally, young people are unlikely to be responsive to those that ignore their concerns.

In the first volume in the Great Questions in Politics series, Morris Fiorina challenges the prominent view that Americans are engaged in a cultural war. In the second volume, Gary Jacobson explores the unprecedented level of partisan polarization that has characterized the presidency of George W. Bush. In *Is Voting for Young People?*, Martin Wattenberg turns the view from passion and polarization to apathy and inactivity.

A prominent scholar of political parties and behavior, Wattenberg focuses his considerable talents on describing and explaining this central feature of contemporary politics. Basing his analysis on systematic data, he provides an authoritative, nuanced, yet clear analysis of young people and politics.

Wattenberg finds that changes in young people's use of the media have resulted in their being far less likely than their elders to be exposed to news about public affairs. One consequence of their relative lack of media exposure is that young people are less likely to follow politics and to appreciate the impact of government on them. Thus, young people see less need to be involved in politics. Even if politicians pay special attention to young adults, it will be difficult for them to reach a generation that pays so little attention to political news.

Equally important, he shows that the political inactivity of young people has important consequences for public policy. The irony of the political inactivity of young people is that in the Unites States and other established democracies, survey evidence shows that more young people voting would make a difference in the election outcomes. The youth vote often favors different candidates and parties than those supported by older generations. By passing up opportunities to vote, young adults cede important decisions to those who have different values and interests.

George C. Edwards III
Texas A & M University

Acknowledgments

This book relies on the cooperation of literally millions of survey respondents over the last six decades. In this era when survey response rates are declining, it bears remembering that so much scholarly research depends on the willingness of randomly chosen individuals to freely give a bit of their time. In addition to these anonymous individuals, I am also grateful to the many scholars who have carried out these studies and generously made them available for others to analyze.

As this project evolved, numerous colleagues provided helpful comments and assistance in gathering data. I wish to especially thank Matthew Beckmann, Russell Dalton, George Edwards, David Farrell, Mark Gray, Hans-Dieter Klingemann, Arend Lijphart, Ian McAllister, Dieter Ohr, Thomas E. Patterson, Andrew Russell, Aiji Tanaka, Carole Uhlaner, and Jack Vowles. Students in my classes at the University of California, Irvine, and the University of New South Wales listened to my ideas on this subject and often helped me to see things from the perspective of their generation.

My original manuscript was given a thorough reading by reviewers Robert Jackson of Florida State University; Martin Johnson of the University of California, Riverside; Miki Kittilson of Arizona State University; Brad Lockerbie of the University of

Georgia; Sean Matheson of Knox College; and Richard Niemi of the University of Rochester. Their helpful comments and suggestions resulted in many substantial improvements in this work.

The hard work of the editorial staff at Pearson Longman proved indispensable. Eric Stano and Donna Garnier kept things moving along smoothly throughout the entire publication process. Elizabeth Jahaske scrutinized every detail of the manuscript, improving the writing throughout and catching a number of oversights and errors. Any errors that may have made it into print are surely my responsibility.

Introduction

"Voting is for Old People," proclaimed a T-shirt printed and distributed in 2004 by Urban Outfitters, a popular American clothing company. At Harvard's Kennedy School of Government, the perceived message of the shirt hit a raw nerve. Its director issued a public statement criticizing the slogan, saying that it could not be further from the truth—that voting is for everyone. In response, Urban Outfitters said they never intended to discourage anyone from voting. Rather, they asserted that their goal was to draw attention to the relative lack of participation of young adults in politics, a problem that many analysts and politicians acknowledge but few seem to be genuinely concerned about. As the clothing company said in a press release, the slogan "Voting is for Old People" was intended "to draw attention to the growing rift between politicians and their platforms and the concerns of young people in this country."[1] Having at least succeeded in drawing attention to their product line, Urban Outfitters soon discontinued the controversial T-shirt, letting the political issue quietly subside.

The central argument of this book is that over the last three decades, politics and voting have indeed become more and more the province of the elderly, which will be shown to be the case not only in the United States but also *throughout the world's advanced industrialized democracies.* There is in fact a rift between politicians and young adults, although not one of mutual contempt but rather of mutual neglect. Many young people don't vote simply because they don't follow politics. Moreover, because so many young people don't follow politics and don't vote, parties and politicians frequently don't bother with young people, thereby further widening the age bias in electoral participation.

All too often, low turnout rates among the young are considered to be a natural part of political life, and hence not worth fretting about. Scholars often write of a life cycle pattern in which people become more aware of the political world as they age, and hence are more likely to vote. As such, it is often thought that today's young nonvoters will eventually show up at the polls and have their voices heard. If such a life cyle truly exists, it ought to be consistently found in: 1) different eras; and 2) across a wide range of democracies. The data examined in this book from a number of countries in the 1970s contradict the life cycle hypothesis. Therefore, the pattern of young people being substantially less likely to follow politics regularly and to vote is a relatively new phenomenon that cries out for an explanation.

The fact that political apathy among young people is now so widespread across the world's established democracies makes it improbable that country-specific factors are at the root of the problem. Americans can reasonably speculate that a series of scandals from Watergate to Monica Lewinsky have turned off successive generations of young adults; Canadians can look to the twin problems of Quebec separatism and Western alienation; the Japanese can perhaps blame the long downturn in their country's economy; Germans can argue that dislocations from the unification process have led young people to turn away from politics; and the list goes on. But these are idiosyncratic reasons for a trend that is widely generalizable. Are we to conclude that it just so happens that various events in most of the world's established democracies have led young people to stay out of politics? When similar changes occur in country after country, we need to search for factors that are reshaping the political environment everywhere.

Communications technology is one such aspect of political life that has undergone transformation throughout the world's advanced industrialized societies—the United States, Western Europe, Japan, Canada, Australia, and New Zealand—in recent years. This book argues that changes in media habits from generation to generation have led to a new situation in which young people are far less likely to be exposed to news about public affairs than their elders. Young adults have not consciously decided to avoid political news in recent years; rather, having been socialized in a markedly different communications environment, they just have not picked up the same media habits that their parents and grandparents did. These media habits, which older people developed long ago in a different world, continue to serve them well in today's political environment—making them substantially more likely to follow politics and become familiar with the issues of the day. And the more one learns about public affairs and follows current events, the more one is likely to realize the stakes involved at the polls.

Because political apathy among young adults stems from their being tuned out from political news, the problem will be particularly difficult to reverse. Even if politicians pay special attention to young adults, it will be difficult for politicians to get through to this generation that pays so little attention to political news. But in actuality, there is very little incentive for politicians to appeal to young adults. Why should they pay any attention to young people if it is so well known that they do not follow political events or vote? Even young adults in the United States seem to be aware of this pattern. A nationwide study of 18- to 24-year-olds conducted by the Center for Information and Research on Civic Learning and Engagement in June 2002 found that 22 percent agreed with the statement that "Most young adults vote." At the same time, 74 percent agreed that "Voting is something older people do." And the consequences of this generation gap in voting were crystal clear to many of these young respondents: sixty-eight percent agreed with the statement that "Politicians care more about the votes of older people than about me." These widely shared sentiments among America's young adults are all essentially correct. This book attempts to establish why these patterns have developed, both in the United States as well as in many other established democracies.

AN OVERVIEW

The first part of this book focuses on the root causes of the generation gap in voter turnout—changes in media consumption habits over time. Chapter 1 examines trends in newspaper reading, demonstrating that over the past three decades, each new cohort of young adults entering the electorate has been less and less likely to have developed the habit of perusing a daily newspaper. This trend is of particular significance because newspapers are by far the best source for learning about politics. Of course, one can learn about politics from other media sources such as television news. But by and large, television is merely a headline delivery service when it comes to politics. Furthermore, Chapter 2 demonstrates that over the past several decades, TV news has become a medium that appeals primarily to older people. When a few networks controlled the airwaves in the broadcasting era, political shows were hard to avoid and reached the young and old alike. In contrast, in the recent era of narrowcasting, young adults have grown up with remote controls in their hands and a plethora of alternatives to politics. Recent data from throughout the established democratic world indicate that when politics is on, young adults are off somewhere else.

With these changes in generational patterns of newspaper reading and TV news watching, the relationship between age and awareness of political events has been dramatically altered. A common saying among young people involved in politics once was that one should never trust anyone over 30. Now, as discussed in Chapter 3, when it comes to current political events and the governmental process, one could well say, "Don't ask anyone under 30," for chances are that they will not be informed. People know what they follow, and politics has unfortunately become a topic that the elderly follow much more closely than do young people. The result is that today's young adults are the least politically knowledgeable generation ever in the history of survey research.

With recent generations establishing modern lows for newspaper reading, TV news watching, and knowledge of public affairs, a significant generation gap has emerged in terms of voter participation in many established democracies. Chapter 4 outlines how getting young adults to vote in presidential and parliamentary elections has become more and more of a problem in the United States and elsewhere. This chapter also examines elections of lesser importance, where the age gap in terms of electoral participation has reached alarming levels in many countries. Chapter 5 then examines generational differences with regard to attitudes about civic duty. These data may well provide a window into the likely future of electoral participation. Because the current generation of young people is relatively unlikely to see voting as an important civic responsibility, many of them may well be lost as voters for the rest of their lives.

By passing up opportunities to vote, young adults are ceding important decisions to those who have different values and interests. Chapter 6 demonstrates that the concerns of young adults differ substantially from those of their elders, with generational differences clearly evident on Left–Right positioning as well as on various policy issues. In the United States and other established democracies, survey evidence from recent elections shows that more young people voting definitely would make a difference because the youth vote often favors different candidates and parties.

Finally, Chapter 7 discusses a variety of reforms that could help ensure that voting is for young people just as much as it is for other age groups. Many good ideas have been proposed that probably would do some good. However, only the institution of compulsory election attendance has proven to be a cure-all for the problem of unequal political participation. Granted, many people may see this as an authoritarian step. Yet, it has worked very successfully in a number of countries, such as Australia, Belgium, and Greece. Given the typical requirements of citizenship such as paying taxes, reporting for jury duty, and registering for potential military service, requiring occasional participation in elections seems to be a relatively small imposition to achieve generational equality at the polls.

CHAPTER I

The Aging of Regular Newspaper Readers

Go any place where a variety of people are waiting around in the morning such as an airport terminal or a train station, and you are likely to observe a now-common behavior pattern: the younger someone is, the less likely he or she is reading a newspaper. It was not always this way. Old movie scenes portray everyone reading newspapers. Young and old alike are shown reading newspapers, as that was how most people got their news. Ever since the 1960s, however, when television supplanted newspapers as the major source of news information, the newspaper business has been fading.

The decline of newspaper consumption has almost completely been due to generational replacement, with each new cohort of young people less likely than its elders to read newspapers. There is little indication of people giving up on newspapers and canceling their subscriptions. Reading a newspaper every day is a habit that, once acquired, is generally continued throughout one's lifetime, and for most people such a routine either is or is not developed by the time a person reaches voting age. What has happened in recent years is that relatively few young adults have picked up this habit.

As with all the major trends outlined in this book, this is not just an American phenomenon. Throughout the established democracies, survey data over time show that regular newspaper readers are now considerably older than was the case in the 1970s. In country after country, the last three decades have seen a transformation of the newspaper from a medium for everyone to an information source primarily for older people.

This worldwide trend would be of little consequence were newspapers being replaced by another source of political information that people could learn as much from. But to date, no viable replacement for newspapers has emerged. One can, of course, learn the basic outline of current events from sources such as CNN's *Headline News*. But this channel is aptly named, as it covers only about what a newspaper reader would get by simply scanning the headlines. If one really wants to be informed about political matters, decades of academic research support the conclusion that newspapers are the best media source.[2]

Over two centuries ago, James Madison foresaw not only the promise of American democracy but also how the then-young medium of newspapers could play a key role in enabling ordinary citizens to participate effectively in democratic governance. As Colleen Sheehan writes, "Madison envisioned newspapers serving as vehicles for circulation of the ideas of the literati to the people of the extensive American republic, resulting in the refinement and enlargement of the public views and the emergence of an enlightened public opinion."[3] Madison would probably be very pleased with the depth of content available in today's newspapers, but disappointed that so many citizens are passing up the opportunity to avail themselves of this wealth of information.

Almost exactly two hundred years after Madison assumed the presidency of the United States, his current successor looks upon newspapers with indifference. In a fall 2003 interview with Brit Hume of *FOX News,* President George W. Bush clearly stated that he didn't read newspapers.[4] This statement led many pundits and scholars to gasp in amazement that a president could ignore such a valuable source of news about the world. Longtime White House correspondent Helen Thomas argued that Bush could hardly claim to be in touch with public opinion if he wasn't reading a newspaper. She wrote that "Anyone who wants to stay in touch with national, international and local events looks forward to reading the newspaper every day. The variety and breadth of newspaper stories make Americans the best-informed people in the world."[5] It should be noted that President Bush maintained that he did not need to read newspapers because his chief of staff and national security advisor provide him with daily news briefings. But this satisfied few critics, who wondered whether even the most trusted aides could be expected to relay a comprehensive sense of the news of the day to the commander in chief.

Left unsaid in this hullabaloo was the hard truth that the percentage of the American public who reads a daily newspaper has been declining for quite some time. Whether Bush's avoidance of newspapers is a good practice for a president or not, the fact that such a large proportion of the population no longer bothers to read a newspaper has made it easier for a president to say he doesn't either. A few decades ago, it probably would have seemed outlandish for the leader of the free world to say this; today, given the decline of newspapers, it is not. This chapter tells the story of how generational change has contributed to this transformation in the United States, as well as in most advanced industrialized democracies.

WHO READS A NEWSPAPER
EVERY DAY ANYMORE?

This chapter's data presentation is premised on the theoretical perspective that newspaper reading is a well-ingrained habit. Data from the 1992–1996 American National Election Panel Study offer strong confirmation for this premise. In both years, the same randomly selected individuals were asked how many days they had read a newspaper in the past week. Sixty-seven percent of respondents who in 1992 had said they read a paper every day said the same thing four years later. In contrast, only 13 percent of the respondents who had said they had not read a paper every day during the past week in 1992 indicated they did so when they were reinterviewed in 1996. The correlation between the actual number of days a respondent said he or she read a newspaper in the past week in 1992 and in 1996 was quite impressive at .64. The stability coefficient for party identification, which is widely regarded as the most stable of all political attitudes, is typically about .80 over four years. Given the disruptions of people's routines that can easily occur in any given week, the fact that responses to the newspaper reading question are nearly as stable as party identification is solid evidence of a deep-rooted habit.

The most straightforward way to present data on newspaper reading routines is to report the percentage who say they read a paper every day of the week. Of course, most people who do not read a paper every day will occasionally pick one up and skim through it. In all likelihood, President Bush sometimes reads a newspaper; when he said he didn't, he probably meant that it wasn't a habit for him. And it is the trends in this habit that we are interested in.

Table 1.1 displays survey data from 1957 to 2004 regarding the percentage of the adult American public who reported reading a newspaper every day of the week. In the late 1950s, surveys indicated that roughly three-quarters of the adult population (then defined as over 21 years of age) read a paper every day. Not shown in the data in Table 1.1 is the fact that this survey asked people how many papers they read as well as how often. Amazingly, 21 percent said they read two papers daily, and another 4 percent said they read three papers every day. Most of these people who read more than one paper a day were probably reading a morning and an afternoon paper. In the absence of the ability to turn on the TV in the evening to get the news, getting a paper that was published in the late afternoon was a good way to keep abreast of late-breaking events. As late as 1970, afternoon papers accounted for 58 percent of daily newspapers sold; by 2001, this figure had fallen to a mere 16 percent.[6]

The survey data show that in the 15 years between 1957 and 1972, there was only a slight decline in daily newspaper reading, though probably far fewer people were reading more than one newspaper a day by the early 1970s. Since the early 1970s,

TABLE 1.1
Percent Reading a Newspaper Every Day of the Week, 1957–2004

Year	Percent
1957	76
1958	75
1967	73
1972	69
1975	67
1977	63
1978	58
1982	53
1983	56
1985	53
1986	54
1987	56
1988	51
1989	50
1990	53
1991	52
1993	47
1994	50
1996	42
1998	43
2000	37
2002	42
2004	41

Sources: 1957 News Media Study; 1958 Omnibus Survey of
Consumer Attitudes and Behavior; 1967 Political Participation
in America Study; 1972–2004 General Social Surveys.

though, the decline in daily newspaper reading has been precipitous. In the 32 years from 1972 to 2004, this habit has declined at the rate of approximately 1 percent a year. Should this trend continue unabated, no one by the year 2045 will be reading a newspaper every day. Of course, such long-term projections can hardly be taken seriously given all the unforeseen factors that might intervene to accelerate or reverse the trend over the next 40 years. But people in the newspaper business are clearly concerned that they are losing customers at a significant and steady rate.[7] Even more alarming for them is the fact that young adults are not reading newspapers at nearly the same rate as previous generations, thereby making it likely that this trend will continue for decades to come.

The generational nature of the decline of daily newspaper reading is dramatically shown in the cohort data displayed in Table 1.2. Looking across the rows, one sees a good deal of stability within each cohort in terms of the percentage reading a newspaper every day. For example, of people born in my cohort (1953–1957), 42 percent in the mid-1970s said they read a newspaper every day, 43 percent in the late 1980s said they did so, and 38 percent in the 2000–2004 period said they did so. This compares poorly to the steady 75 percent rate of daily newspaper reading among my parents' cohort. Such a generational difference is hardly unusual; Table 1.2 clearly shows that since the beginning of the TV age, new cohorts have been less likely to report reading a newspaper every day. Thus, the routine of reading a newspaper every day is not evident at nearly the same rate among new cohorts as compared to the age groups that are currently dying out. At present, seven out of ten of the most elderly adults have

TABLE 1.2
Cohort Analysis of Percent Reading the Newspaper Every Day

BORN IN:	2000–2004	1987–1989	1972–1977	1967	1957
1978–1982	20				
1973–1977	19				
1968–1972	26	22			
1963–1967	31	30			
1958–1962	33	37			
1953–1957	38	43	42		
1948–1952	46	53	50		
1943–1947	50	58	56	57	
1938–1942	55	57	65	64	
1933–1937	62	65	72	75	70*
1928–1932	72	66	74	79	74
1923–1927		74	79	75	78
1918–1922		74	79	79	76
1913–1917		72	79	77	82
1908–1912			78	79	80
1903–1907			79	76	82
1898–1902			77	78	77
1893–1897				75	75

*Only 1933 to 1936 here

Sources: 1957 News Media Study; 1967 Political Participation in America Study; 1972–2004 General Social Surveys.

read a newspaper every day throughout their lives. In contrast, among the young adults who are replacing them in the electorate, only about two in ten have thus far developed this media consumption habit.

Has Reading a Newspaper for Political Content Changed?

Newspapers are an incredibly diverse source of information on all sorts of topics—politics, sports, weather, business, culture, health, etc. Therefore, it cannot be assumed that people who read a newspaper every day are actually taking in the political news. They may well subscribe to a daily newspaper in order to check out one or two sections of the newspaper that have nothing to do with politics. In the era before television news, it may well have been the case that young people picked up a newspaper only because it was the primary means for checking the weather and sports scores. Fortunately, the Survey Research Center's 1957 and 1958 media usage surveys asked about the types of newspaper stories people usually read. Table 1.3 presents the data by age group from these late-1950s surveys regarding reading stories about national politics. Respondents who were under 30 years old were somewhat less likely than other age groups to say that they read all the way through the national political news. On the other hand, seniors were a bit more likely to report that they never read a newspaper at all. Overall, the correlation between age and level of attention to political stories in the newspaper was a mere .03. In sum, young, middle aged, and old alike took in newspaper coverage of national politics at about the same rate.

Unfortunately, there are no recent survey data specifically on newspaper consumption of national political stories. The best available time-series data are from the American National Election Studies (ANES), which have continually

TABLE 1.3
Frequency of Reading about National Politics by Age, 1957–1958 (in percents)

	READ ALL	READ SOME	GLANCE AT	SKIP OVER	NEVER READ THE PAPER
21–29	16	37	20	18	9
30–44	24	37	18	14	7
45–64	22	38	16	15	9
65+	27	30	12	17	14

Question wording: "How often do you read the newspapers?" (If at all), "Of course, all people aren't interested in the same things in the paper, so I would like to get an idea of the kinds of things that interest you in the paper. Would you tell me about how often you usually read each kind of news—do you read it all the way through, read some of it, just glance at it, or skip over it?" How about "stories about national politics"?

Source: Combined data from 1957 U.S. Media Study and Spring 1958 U.S. Survey of Consumer Attitudes and Behavior.

asked respondents whether they read about the presidential campaign in the newspaper or not. Table 1.4 presents these data by age group for the period from 1960 to 2004. From 1960 to 1976, there was no consistent difference in this measure between the youngest and oldest citizens. Since 1980, though, those under 30 have been substantially less likely to pick up a newspaper and read about the presidential race. In both 1996 and 2000, senior citizens were more than twice as likely to say that they had read campaign articles in newspapers compared to people under 30. The ANES data clearly confirm that not only is newspaper readership down sharply among young adults but also that today's youth are much less likely to follow politics in the newspaper than their parents and grandparents were at the same age.

TABLE 1.4

Percent Reading Newspapers about the Campaign by Age, 1960–2004

	18–29	30–44	45–64	65+	DIFFERENCE BETWEEN 65+ AND <30
1960	84	80	81	74	+10
1964	75	80	80	77	−2
1968	68	81	76	72	−4
1972	49	59	62	61	−11
1976	68	78	77	70	−2
1980	56	78	76	72	−16
1984	62	77	77	70	−8
1988	35	47	57	57	−22
1992	35	50	57	60	−25
1996	28	39	52	60	−32
2000	27	35	48	56	−29
2004	34	39	51	61	−27

Question wording: 1952–1976: "We're interested in this interview in finding out whether people paid much attention to the election campaign this year. Take newspapers for instance–did you read about the campaign in any newspaper?"; 1980–1984: "Did you read about the campaign in any newspapers?"; 1988–2004: "How many days in the past week did you read a daily newspaper?" (If R has read a daily newspaper in the past week:) "Did you read about the campaign in any newspaper?"

Source: American National Election Studies.

CAN SIMILAR PATTERNS BE FOUND IN OTHER ESTABLISHED DEMOCRACIES?

If competition from television is the principal reason why younger Americans have not gotten into the newspaper reading habit, then similar generational patterns should be found throughout much of the world. Even tiny, isolated Bhutan now has television service, and as a result has seen its way of life transformed.[8] If television has had that sort of effect in Bhutan, then it is a fairly safe assumption that other advanced industrialized democracies like the United States will have experienced similar effects. On the other hand, if newspapers continue to appeal to young people in other countries, then the American pattern must stem from something particular about the quality or appeal of American newspapers, or the nature of American politics.

In order to assess whether other countries have experienced the same generational patterns as the United Staes, one needs cross-national data on the regularity of newspaper reading in many countries from different eras. Various data exist for a number of countries, but for the sake of comparability it is best to look to collaborative studies that have asked identically worded questions at roughly the same time in a wide range of countries. The earliest data I could find in a cross-national study was the 1981–1983 World Values Study, which asked respondents throughout much of the world whether they regularly read a daily newspaper. Table 1.5 displays the results from this question by age category in the United States and 12 other established democracies. These results show that as of the early 1980s, the correlation between age and regular newspaper reading in the United States was roughly in line with what was found in other democracies. In 10 of the 13 countries, there was only slight evidence of younger people being less likely to read newspapers frequently. The three exceptions were France, where young people were much less likely to read a paper, and Ireland and Italy, where senior citizens were actually the least likely to be habitual newspaper consumers.

For a current-day comparison, the best available data in a cross-national study can be found in the 2002/3 European Social Survey,

TABLE 1.5

Percent Who Regularly Read a Newspaper by Age
in 13 Countries in the Early 1980s

	18–29	30–44	45–64	65+	DIFFERENCE BETWEEN 65+ AND 18–29	CORRELATION WITH AGE
FRANCE	34	42	60	69	+35	.25
GERMANY	72	84	89	86	+14	.17
USA	61	70	78	75	+14	.12
CANADA	59	68	70	72	+13	.09
NETHERLANDS	82	88	93	90	+8	.10
UK	76	80	91	83	+7	.10
DENMARK	82	87	90	88	+6	.07
SWEDEN	90	96	98	96	+6	.07
JAPAN	75	89	88	79	+4	.07
BELGIUM	55	61	62	59	+4	.05
NORWAY	92	95	99	94	+2	.08
IRELAND	78	80	75	66	−12	−.08
ITALY	47	58	44	32	−15	−.09

Question wording: "Do you regularly read a daily newspaper? That is, at least 4 out of every 6 issues?"

Source: 1981–1983 World Values Study.

which asked respondents how much time they spent reading a paper on an average weekday. As shown in Table 1.6, the relationship between age and frequency of newspaper reading was much higher in these recent survey data. Of the countries covered by the recent European Social Survey, nine were also included in the World Values Study of the early 1980s. On average, senior citizens in these countries were 10 percent less likely to classify themselves as regular

TABLE 1.6

Percent of Europeans Who Read a Newspaper for at Least 30 Minutes on a Typical Weekday in 2002–2003

	18–29	30–44	45–64	65+	DIFFERENCE BETWEEN 65+ AND 18–29	CORRELATION WITH AGE*
DENMARK	18	29	52	72	+54	.42
GERMANY	28	37	58	74	+46	.34
SWEDEN	37	42	65	80	+43	.36
FINLAND	39	46	63	80	+41	.36
SWITZERLAND	35	44	60	75	+40	.31
NETHERLANDS	39	40	64	75	+36	.33
NORWAY	50	58	78	86	+36	.32
FRANCE	21	24	37	51	+30	.20
BELGIUM	26	30	38	54	+28	.22
AUSTRIA	37	43	54	65	+28	.21
UK	43	40	52	65	+23	.22
IRELAND	48	50	66	70	+22	.15
ITALY	30	35	37	32	+2	.03

Question wording: "On an average weekday, how much time, in total, do you spend reading the newspapers?"

*For the correlations, responses to the newspaper question are recoded into approximate number of minutes as follows: no time at all = 0; less than $1/_2$ hour = 15; $1/_2$ hour to 1 hour = 45; more than 1 hour, up to $1^1/_2$ hours = 75; more than $1^1/_2$ hours, up to 2 hours = 105; more than 2 hours, up to $2^1/_2$ hours = 135; more than $2^1/_2$ hours, up to 3 hours = 165; more than 3 hours = 195.

Source: European Social Survey, 2002/3.

newspaper readers in recent surveys than in the early 1980s. In contrast, respondents under 30 years of age were 38 percent less likely to meet the criteria for regular newspaper readership in the 2002–2003 period than young people in the same countries had been two decades earlier. The result is a clear increase in the relationship between age and frequent newspaper reading in every country for which data are available over the past two decades.

Germany provides an especially clear example of this phenomenon. In both Tables 1.5 and 1.6, Germany ranks second in terms of the relationship between age and newspaper reading. In the early 1980s, though, there was only a slight tendency for younger Germans to be less likely to read newspapers—72 percent of Germans under 30 said they regularly read a newspaper compared to between 84 and 89 percent among the other age categories. By 2002, one can see a strong linear pattern in the German survey data, with only 28 percent of Germans under 30 reporting that they read a paper for at least 30 minutes a day compared to 74 percent among German senior citizens.

Ireland presents another good example. Like Germany, Ireland's rank in terms of the correlation between age and reading a paper on a regular basis was the same at both time points, being relatively weak in both tables. In the early 1980s, the only substantial difference in newspaper reading habits by age in Ireland was that senior citizens were actually the least likely to be regular readers. Two decades later, however, senior citizens were clearly the most likely to read newspapers, with 70 percent saying they spent at least 30 minutes with one on a typical day compared to just 48 percent among young adults.

Cross-national data with regard to reading newspapers specifically for political news also show clear evidence of the aging of the newspaper audience. The World Values Study did not ask such a question, but fortunately this is available for eight nations in the 1973–1976 Political Action study. Table 1.7 presents by age

TABLE 1.7

Percent Who Read about Politics in the Newspaper Often or Sometimes in Eight Countries, 1973–1976

	18–29	30–44	45–64	65+	DIFFERENCE BETWEEN 65+ AND 18–29	CORRELATION WITH AGE*
NETHERLANDS	58	70	65	71	+13	.07
USA	66	81	81	73	+7	.09
UK	62	68	70	67	+5	.09
SWITZERLAND	58	70	71	63	+5	.04
AUSTRIA	56	59	60	57	+1	.04
FINLAND	63	62	64	63	0	.04
GERMANY	72	76	75	67	−5	.00
ITALY	54	37	32	25	−29	−.23

Question wording: "How often do you read about politics in the newspapers: often, sometimes, seldom, or never?"

*Responses to the newspaper question were recoded as follows for the correlations: often = 100; sometimes = 67; seldom = 33; never = 0.

Source: Political Action: An Eight Nation Study, 1973–1976.

category the percentage in each country who reported that they often or sometimes read about politics[9] in the newspapers, as well as correlations summarizing how closely these two variables were related. Both the correlations and the percentages indicate that in the mid-1970s, there was only a slight tendency in most of these countries for older people to read newspaper stories about politics more frequently than younger people did so. The exception is Italy, where young Italians of the 1970s—the only group not to have experienced any of the Mussolini era—were substantially more likely to be reading about politics in the newspapers.

TABLE 1.8

Percent of Europeans Who Read a Daily Newspaper at Least
30 Minutes to Learn about Politics in 2002–2003

	18–29	30–44	45–64	65+	DIFFERENCE BETWEEN 65+ AND <30	CORRELATION WITH AGE*
DENMARK	8	15	28	48	+40	.33
NORWAY	20	24	40	53	+33	.28
FINLAND	12	17	28	45	+33	.29
SWITZERLAND	11	17	29	41	+30	.23
NETHERLANDS	14	19	29	42	+28	.23
SWEDEN	11	13	26	36	+25	.25
GERMANY	10	13	23	35	+25	.24
IRELAND	20	24	41	44	+24	.17
UK	11	13	17	28	+17	.16
AUSTRIA	18	18	28	33	+15	.15
FRANCE	12	12	20	24	+12	.12
BELGIUM	11	11	18	22	+11	.11
ITALY	11	14	20	20	+9	.08

Question wording: "On an average weekday, how much time, in total, do you spend reading
the newspapers? And how much of this time is spent reading about politics and current affairs?"

* For the correlations, responses to the newspaper question are recoded into approximate
number of minutes as follows: no time at all = 0; less than $1/_2$ hour = 15; $1/_2$ hour to
1 hour = 45; more than 1 hour, up to $1^1/_2$ hours = 75; more than $1^1/_2$ hours, up to
2 hours = 105; more than 2 hours, up to $2^1/_2$ hours = 135; more than $2^1/_2$ hours, up
to 3 hours = 165; more than 3 hours = 195.

Source: European Social Survey, 2002/3.

Today, young people in all the established European democracies are significantly less prone to spend a fair amount of time
reading about politics in the newspaper, as demonstrated by the
data displayed in Table 1.8. All the European countries for

which we can compare current patterns to those from the 1970s show a notable increase in the correlation between age and reading newspaper stories about public affairs. In the mid-1970s Political Action data (Table 1.7), this correlation averaged .01 in the seven European countries (or .05 if excluding Italy). In the recent European Social Survey data, the relationship in these same countries had increased to an average of .20 (or .22 if excluding Italy).[10]

In sum, the evidence clearly supports the conclusion that the pattern of aging audiences reading political stories in newspapers is quite common throughout the world's established democracies. Newspapers have become more and more for the elderly. And if young citizens are to learn about politics, it seems that it will have to be from some other media. Young people throughout the world's advanced industrialized democracies have simply not gotten into the routine of picking up a daily newspaper and reading about current events.

Do Young Adults Just Not Like to Read?

One possible explanation for why recent generations have not gotten into the newspaper reading habit may be that they are simply less fond of reading. Growing up with TV, computers, and video games may have created a markedly different socialization process in which reading plays a significantly smaller role in their lives. If this is the case, then the age-related trends we have found for newspaper consumption might be seen as part of a general societal failure to instill an appreciation for reading in recent generations.

Yet, although this seems to be a sensible hypothesis, the available survey evidence is not at all supportive of it.

Contrary to any notion that socialization has come to be less centered around books, the 2000 U.S. General Social Survey found that today's young adults grew up with more books around the house than previous generations. This survey asked respondents how many books there were around their homes when they were 16 years old. Two-thirds of respondents under the age of 30 said that there had been at least 50 books around their homes, compared to 56 percent among those between the ages of 30 and 64, and 36 percent among senior citizens. The greater availability of books during the socialization of younger people probably reflects the increase in American education levels over the years.

As the overall level of education has increased over the past half century, Americans have in fact become more likely to say that they read books. Fifty-seven percent of respondents interviewed in the 2002 national survey of Public Participation in the Arts said they had read a book in the past year compared to just 35 percent of respondents in the 1957 News Media Study. In both studies, young people were actually slightly more likely to report having read a book than older people, but in both cases the relationship between age and reading books was insignificant once education was controlled for.[11]

Data over time are not available from other countries, but recent surveys show that the current American pattern is typical. In August/September 2001, the Eurobarometer asked people in the European Economic Community whether they had read a book for reasons other than for work or school in the last year.

The correlation between age and reading a book for pleasure ranged from −.13 in Italy to .05 in the United Kingdom, averaging a mere −.02 in the 11 established democracies where the question was asked. Similarly, in the 2000 Japanese Social Survey, the correlation between age and whether or not respondents said they usually read at least one book in a month was −.06. In sum, these slightly negative correlations indicate that young adults in established democracies are slightly more likely to read books than their elders. Today's young adults do in fact read—they just don't usually read newspapers.

Conclusion: A Future for Newspapers?

The financial viability of the printed newspaper being delivered to one's front door every morning is therefore surely in doubt. Many people believe that the future of the newspaper business lies with the Internet. Today, most major newspapers have an online edition. It is certainly conceivable that as a younger generation accustomed to receiving news electronically comes of age, the newspaper business will make a successful transition to an Internet-based medium. Available survey data from the United States and Europe do show that the younger someone is, the more likely he or she is to read newspaper articles online. But this pattern probably stems simply from younger people's greater computer literacy. There is little indication that reading newspapers online has yet become an important facet of the Internet experience for many people.

Indeed, the frequency with which even young adults go to newspaper Web sites has thus far been relatively unimpressive. A May 2004 Pew survey found that only 7 percent of respondents under 30 years old said that they regularly read "the websites of major national newspapers such as the *USA Today.com, New York Times.com,* or the *Wall Street Journal* online." Of course, one doesn't have to go to the sites of prestigious national newspapers for the Internet to take the place of a traditional newspaper, as virtually every local paper now has a presence on the Web. Fortunately, this study also asked people whether they regularly read "the websites of your local newspaper or TV stations." Given that most TV station Web sites are rudimentary and that TV covers breaking news live as opposed to posting information, it seems reasonable to assume that most respondents had newspapers in mind when they responded to this question. All told, only 9 percent of young adults said they used such sites regularly, and many of them also said that they frequently read the sites of national newspapers and therefore would appear to be news hounds.

In Europe, the experience thus far with newspaper Web sites has been relatively similar. The August/September 2001 Eurobarometer asked people what they usually used the Internet for, providing "reading articles on the websites of newspapers" as one possible response. Overall, just 8 percent of adult citizens in the European Economic Community said they usually did so; Europeans between the ages of 18 and 29 led the way with 13 percent of them regularly reading newspapers online.

In sum, newspaper Web sites have a long way to go in order to take the place of the printed page as a source of political information. Today's young adults can potentially learn a tremendous amount about politics from newspaper Web sites, *if they so choose,* but it would appear that very few are choosing to do so.

One might ponder the findings of this chapter and conclude that although television will never provide as much detailed information as newspapers do, at least young adults can partially make up for their lack of interest in newspapers by watching TV news. However, as will be seen in the next chapter, when politics is on television, young people are more likely than ever to tune out.

CHAPTER 2

The Aging Audience for Politics on TV

It didn't take long after the start of television broadcasting for newspapers to realize the potential competition they were facing. In fact, one of the reasons *TV Guide* became a top-selling publication was that many newspapers would not print television schedules for fear of the competition from the new medium. By the late 1950s, astute politicians were realizing the potential of television. A year before he was elected president, John F. Kennedy wrote in an article for *TV Guide* about the impact TV was already having, arguing that "TV has altered drastically the nature of our political campaigns, conventions, constituents, candidates, and costs."[12] The revolutionary effect of television on politics was evident to Hollywood early on as well. In the classic 1958 movie *The Last Hurrah*, Spencer Tracy's character urges his nephew to follow him along on the campaign trail to witness a traditional campaign while he still can. Tracy's lines go as follows:

> *It's my guess that the old-fashioned political campaign in a few years will be as extinct as the dodo. It will all be TV. . . . Mind you, I use the TV sometimes, but I also get out into the wards. I speak in arenas, armories, street corners, anywhere I can get a crowd. I even kiss babies. . . . But there's no use kidding myself—it is on the way out.*

While this prediction now seems prophetic, it also tells us just how clear it was to those who lived through the early years of television that politics was being rapidly transformed.

For political scientists, though, the impact of television on politics was long considered to be minimal. This conclusion was especially prevalent with regard to learning about political issues. For example, Patterson and McClure's classic study of the 1972 U.S. presidential election, aptly titled *The Unseeing Eye*, concluded that the networks "may have allowed Americans to 'see' the campaign, but in so doing they have added nothing of substance to the voters' civic education."[13] The widely acknowledged superficiality of television news coverage for quite some time led scholars to largely ignore the impact the medium was having on politics.

Another reason that so much early scholarship regarding television and politics fit under the rubric of "minimal effects" is that most of these studies were looking for direct impacts—for example, whether the media influenced how people voted.[14] When the focus turned to how the media affect *what Americans think about*, more impressive results were uncovered. In a series of controlled laboratory experiments, Shanto Iyengar and Donald Kinder subtly manipulated the stories that participants saw on the TV news.[15] They found that they could significantly affect the importance people attached to a given problem by splicing a few stories about it into the news over the course of a week. Iyengar and Kinder do not maintain that the networks can make something out of nothing or conceal problems that actually exist. But they do conclude that "what television news does, instead, is alter the priorities Americans attach to a circumscribed set of problems, all of which are plausible contenders for public concern."[16] Subsequent research by Miller and Krosnick has revealed that agenda setting effects are particularly strong among politically knowledgeable citizens who trust the media. Thus, rather than television news manipulating the public, they argue that agenda setting reflects a deliberate and thoughtful process on the part of sophisticated citizens who rely on an information source they have come to trust.[17]

But who are these viewers whose receptiveness to the messages conveyed by TV news are the ones setting the public agenda? All too often, it is assumed that they are representative of the public at large because of the vast size of the audience reached by major broadcast networks. Such an assumption may well have been valid in the era when a few networks dominated the market in the United States and other established democracies. However, in today's world of a plethora of television channels, the representativeness of the TV news audience can no longer be taken for granted. As this chapter will show, the audience for TV news has become increasingly skewed toward the elderly in recent decades. When politics is on, young people are off somewhere else, or are reaching for the remote control. Moreover, as with the findings regarding newspapers, data over time show that such generational differences were not always the case.

Central to any generational phenomenon are changes in socialization experiences. Since the early 1980s, young people have been socialized in a rapidly changing media environment that has been radically different from that experienced by the past couple of generations. The first major American networks—ABC, NBC, and CBS—adopted the term "broadcasting" in the names of their companies because their signal was being sent out to a broad audience. When these networks dominated the industry, each had to deal with general topics that the public as a whole was concerned with such as politics and government. However, with the development of cable and satellite TV, market segmentation has taken hold. Sports buffs can watch ESPN all day; music buffs can tune to MTV or VH1; history buffs can glue their dial to the History Channel; and so forth. Rather than appealing to a general audience, channels such as ESPN, MTV, and C-SPAN focus on a narrow, particular interest. Hence, their mission has often been termed "narrowcasting," rather than the traditional "broadcasting."

Because of the narrowcasting revolution, today's youth have grown up in an environment in which public affairs news has not been as readily visible as it was in the past. Major political events were once shared national experiences. However, the current generation of young adults is the first to grow up in a media environment in which there are few such shared experiences. As channels have proliferated, it has become much easier to avoid exposure to politics altogether by simply grabbing the remote control. It has become particularly difficult for political programming on television to get through to a generation who has channel surfed all their lives. This chapter tells the story of how young people have come to tune out politics on TV, both in the United States as well as in most established democracies.

Is Network TV News a Dying Dinosaur?

For a time, the anchors of the three nightly news broadcasts were major figures in American political life. As Jeff Alan writes, "For all of us who grew up with the evening news anchors in our living rooms and family rooms five nights a week, it's fair to say that we saw more of the anchors than we saw of most of our neighbors, and even some of our close friends and relatives."[18] In 1974, the American National Election Study actually asked people to rate news anchors on a feeling thermometer scale ranging from 0 to 100, just as they did for major political leaders. Respondents were told that if they did not recognize a name, or felt they could not rate that individual, just to say so. All but 7 percent were able to rate Walter Cronkite of CBS, and all but 17 percent rated John Chancellor of NBC and Howard K. Smith of ABC. By comparison, 39 percent could not rate Senator Jackson, 52 percent could not rate Senator Mondale, and 65 percent could not rate Senator Bentsen—all of whom were prominent senators gearing up for a run at the presidency. By the end of 1980, one could make a legitimate argument that network newscasts had played a significant role in the political downfall of Presidents Johnson, Nixon, and Carter due to the way the newscasts drew attention to those presidents' shortcomings. As Barbara Matusow wrote about the stars of the evening news in 1983, "They have taken their place beside presidents, congressmen, labor leaders, industrialists, and others who shape public policy and private attitudes."[19]

Over the last quarter century, however, the NBC, CBS, and ABC nightly news broadcasts have gone from being instrumental in setting the nation's agenda, to the TV equivalent of dinosaurs on their last legs. During the 1968–1969 TV season, the combined audience of these three news programs on a typical evening was an incredible 50 percent of the American public. At about this time, Walter Cronkite was often called "the most trusted man in America." Thus, when Cronkite's view on the Vietnam War turned negative after the 1968 Tet Offensive, President Johnson quite reasonably concluded that if he had lost Cronkite's support, then he could no longer count on the support of the American people. Today, if a TV news anchor were to come out against the Iraq War, President Bush would hardly be likely to take much notice. None of today's news anchors enjoys anything approaching the audience share that Cronkite long enjoyed. As can be seen in the Nielsen ratings displayed in Table 2.1, the combined rating of the three network broadcasts has steadily declined from 50 in 1968–1969 to just 20 in 2003–2004. As New York Times media critic Frank Rich recently wrote, "The No. 1 cliché among media critics is that we're watching the 'last hurrah' of network news anchors as we have known them for nearly half a century."[20]

It doesn't take much analytical ability these days to recognize that the network news broadcasts are barely hanging on, relying on older viewers who got into the habit of viewing these shows decades ago. Just as one can easily guess the demographics of people most likely to watch the Super Bowl by noting the many advertisements for beer and chips, so one can easily see that the

TABLE 2.1
The Decline in Ratings of U.S. National Network Evening News, 1980–2004

1968–1969* (ALL-TIME HIGH)	50
1980–1981	37
1981–1982	36
1982–1983	35
1983–1984	33
1984–1985	33
1985–1986	34
1986–1987	31
1987–1988	30
1988–1989	29
1989–1990	29
1990–1991	28
1991–1992	28
1992–1993	28
1993–1994	28
1994–1995	26
1995–1996	24
1996–1997	23
1997–1998	23
1998–1999	22
1999–2000	24
2000–2001	23
2001–2002	22
2002–2003	21
2003–2004	20

* The 1968–1969 ratings are inferred through the information provided in *The State of the News Media, 2005,* which shows that the three nightly newscasts have seen their ratings decline by 59 percent from their peak in the 1968–1969 season.

Sources: 1980–1999, *Report on Television* (New York: Nielsen Media Research, 2000), p. 21; 1969 & 2000–2003, *The State of the News Media, 2005* (posted at http://www.stateofthemedia.org/2005/index.asp) (accessed March 14, 2005).

network news audience is quite elderly by keeping an eye on the ads. For example, on one randomly chosen night (January 13, 2004), the CBS *Nightly News* was interspersed with commercials for the following products: Pepto Bismol, Ambien, Ex-Lax, Pepcid Complete, Imitrex, Ester-C, Dulcolax, Maalox, Wellbutrin XL, Detrol LA, and Benefiber. If one doesn't know what some of these products are, one is probably best off that way—suffice it to say that these ads are not for anything that one would buy for pleasure. Even products that could theoretically appeal to all age groups were advertised so as to appeal to senior citizens. An ad for dinner rolls from Pillsbury featured an elderly couple who raved about how the package allowed them to use only a few at a time, which was great now that their kids had moved out. Coricidon was portrayed not just as a cold remedy but also as a treatment appropriate for someone with high blood pressure. And Quaker Oatmeal was described as a good food to reduce cholesterol.

The generational nature of the decline of the network TV news is clearly shown in the cohort data from 1967, 1984, and 2004 displayed in Table 2.2. Overall, these surveys show that the percentage of the public who said they watched a network news broadcast every night was 72 percent in 1967, 45 percent in 1984, and 29 percent in 2004. This rate of decline almost perfectly parallels the trend found in the Nielsen ratings, thereby lending added confidence in the results of these surveys. Unlike the case with newspaper reading habits, the magnitude of this decline has been so great that it is apparent that over the years, some people within each cohort have gotten out of the routine of watching the network news every night. The fact that older people got into the habit of regularly watching these broadcasts during their heyday

TABLE 2.2

Cohort Analysis of Percent Watching U.S. Evening Network TV News on a Daily Basis

	2004	1984	1967
BORN IN:			
1983–1986	8	—	—
1973–1982	15	—	—
1963–1972	21	24	—
1953–1962	28	28	—
1943–1952	42	35	64
1933–1942	47	51	68
1923–1932	52	62	69
1913–1922	—	67	73
1903–1912	—	70	76
1893–1902	—	—	79
1882–1892	—	—	79

Question wording: 1967: "How often do you watch the news broadcasts on TV—every day, a few times a week, about once a week, less than once a week, or never?"; 1984: "How often do you watch the national network news on TV—every day, 3 or 4 times a week, once or twice a week, or less often?"; 2004: "How many days in the past week did you watch the national network news on TV?"

Sources: 1967 Political Participation in America Study; 1984 and 2004 U.S. National Election Studies.

has left senior citizens as the primary audience for such shows today. In 1967, there was relatively little variation in news viewing habits by age, and TV news producers could hardly write off young adults, given that roughly two out of three said they had watched such broadcasts every night. In contrast, by 2004 senior citizens were four times more likely than those under 30 to say that they had watched the network news every night in the past week. Nielsen Media Research reported that the median age of viewers of the *CBS, ABC,* and *NBC News* from September 2003 through early February 2004 was almost exactly 60 years of age—18 years older than the audience for a typical prime-time program.[21] Perhaps more than any other genre of programming, network news has become television for "old people."

A Pew Research Center survey from January 2004 casts further light on young adults' relative lack of reliance on broadcast news programs. Respondents were asked how often, if ever, they learned something about the presidential campaign or the candidates from a variety of media sources. Among respondents under 30 years old, 23 percent said they regularly learned something from network newscasts as compared to 21 percent from comedy TV shows. Commenting on this survey finding, Jon Stewart of the *Daily Show* at first dismissed out of hand any notion that young people were turning to his comedy show to learn about political events. Lately, his show has adopted the slogan of "Keeping America Informed—Unintentionally." If young Americans are putting such inadvertent learning from comedy shows on par with what they get from the nightly network news, then clearly they are not getting much from the traditional NBC, CBS, and ABC broadcasts.

IS CABLE NEWS PICKING UP THE SLACK?

Of course, viewers now have an alternative to the 30-minute network news shows in the form of a round-the-clock news on CNN, MSNBC, and the FOX News Channel. The 24-hour format of cable news is especially well suited to the lifestyle of younger people, who are more likely to be constantly on the go with ever-changing schedules. Data from the 2004 Pew Research Center's media consumption study bear out this point. This survey asked a national sample the following question: "Are you more the kind of person who watches or listens to the news at regular times, or are you more the kind of person who checks in on the news from time to time?" Sixty-five percent of respondents under the age of 30 chose the latter option, compared to 45 percent among people between the ages of 30 and 64, and just 33 percent among senior citizens. Given how cable news is so compatible with young adults' flexible daily schedules, it should come as little surprise to find that the under-30 crowd is far more likely to say that they learn more about politics from these channels than from the broadcast networks.[22]

On the positive side, there can be little doubt that there is a good deal of *potential* for learning about politics from watching the seemingly endless supply of political coverage from cable news channels. This potential is nicely illustrated by one finding from the Pew Research Center's January 2004 study of political engagement and media usage. Among the 7 percent of respondents who scored highest on political engagement—those who said they followed the campaign closely, enjoyed following it, and were familiar with all the campaign events and facts that the survey asked about—cable news was the news source they most frequently relied upon for information about the campaign.[23] If one is truly motivated to follow all the ins and outs of political life, then around-the-clock cable news channels provide far more opportunities than ever before in the history of television.

Yet, it is important to note that the potential of cable news is often not realized in practice. Although these channels have seemingly unlimited opportunities to cover political events and issues, their resources are far from up to the task. Political scientist William Taubman experienced the constraints of cable news firsthand when he served as CNN's expert analyst during the Reagan-Gorbachev summit in 1988. Taubman "thought of the all-news network as having twenty-four hours a day to play with" and proposed numerous interviews with Soviet citizens about their country's struggle to transform itself. However, he soon found that CNN thought of itself as having "forty-eight half-hour segments, each of which had to cover the world and pay for that coverage with regularly scheduled features."[24] Of the numerous interviews he recommended, only a few were done, each lasting just a couple minutes. And when Taubman was on the air, it usually wasn't long before he heard the dreaded words of "Wrap it up and head for commercial" in his earpiece.

William Taubman's experience is instructive as to the shortcomings of cable news. A recent content analysis of CNN, FOX News, and MSNBC programming confirms just how little substantive information is usually conveyed via cable news channels. Columbia University's Project for Excellence in Journalism analyzed 240 hours of cable news programming during 2003. Their report on this content analysis provides a telling indictment of the medium. Among their many findings were that: 1) only 11 percent of the time was taken up with written and edited stories; 2) the role of the reporter was primarily to talk extemporaneously; 3) stories were repeated frequently, usually without any important new information; and 4) coverage of the news was spotty, ignoring many important topics. Network news may well still fit Patterson and McClure's description of "the unseeing eye," but the Columbia study is even less flattering to cable news, aptly labeling much of it as simply "talk radio on television."[25] As media critic Thomas Rosenstiel writes, "Network journalism originally was designed not to make a profit but to create prestige. Cable is all about profit and keeping costs low. What is disappearing is an idealism about the potential of TV as a medium to better our politics and society."[26]

In sum, more people—particularly young adults—may say that cable news is their primary source of political information, but there is good reason to be skeptical about how much the *typical* person with only limited political interest actually absorbs from these channels. The combined rating for the three hour-long news shows on cable (*Newsnight* on CNN, *Special Report* on FOX News, and *Countdown* on MSNBC) was a miniscule 2.3 as of January 2005. Thus, the audience size of these programs is a mere tenth of that of the NBC, ABC, and CBS programs. Given that so few people watch an entire news program on the cable news channels, and that most people say they rely on these channels for political information, this means that they tune in only occasionally during a spare moment. It is unlikely that these channels are the source for much detailed learning about politics. In particular, the fact that young people are relying on cable news as opposed to network news probably means that they are just getting quick snippets as opposed to full stories that could allow them to grasp the details.

WHERE HAVE ALL THE WATER-COOLER SHOWS GONE?

One of the theoretical strengths of cable news is that it provides live coverage of political events whenever they occur. Young adults today have grown up in a media environment in which it has been possible to see far more live events than ever before. For example, cable news channels now show the president live almost anytime he deems to speak in front of TV cameras. However, there is a big difference between having opportunities and taking advantage of them. The range of programming options in the narrowcasting era is so extensive that it allows one to keep one's viewing to a limited range of interests. Whereas once it was difficult to avoid major political events like a state of the union address or a presidential nominating convention, in the narrowcasting age it is a simple matter of reaching for a remote control, or turning to a videotape or DVD. Growing up in a fragmented media environment with scores of TV channels and thousands of movies at the local Blockbuster has offered today's youth a rich and varied socialization experience, but also one that has enabled them to easily avoid political events.

One result of the narrowcasting revolution has been the near extinction of what the television industry calls "water-cooler shows." Such shows were so widely watched that workers who met at the office water cooler the next day could easily strike up a conversation by talking about a program that most people had seen. When there were only a few shows on TV at any given time, one show would often pull in a huge audience; today, with all the competition each show faces, the chances that one show will get a big share of viewers have been greatly reduced. An examination of Nielsen Media Research's list of the one hundred most popular shows from 1960 to 2000 illustrates this point nicely. Excluding live sporting events (which make up one-third of the list), only three shows since 1984 made the list—the finales of *Cheers*, *Seinfeld*, and *The Cosby Show.* In contrast, 16 different episodes of *The Beverly Hillbillies* from the early 1960s were on the list. To this day, the episode where Granny mistakes a kangaroo for a giant jackrabbit remains the highest-rated half-hour program since the current Nielsen system began in 1960.

Political events used to fit the bill of water-cooler shows quite frequently. If Nielsen had included events that were broadcast on multiple networks in their list, then political events would have figured prominently. For example, the typical rating that Presidents Nixon, Ford, and Carter received when they appeared on TV to give speeches or hold a press conference was 48—a higher rating than even the most popular *Beverly Hillbillies* episode. Of course, the huge audience share that political events often garnered was not due to their riveting appeal but rather to the simple fact that there used to be little in the way of viewing alternatives when regular programming on CBS, NBC, and ABC was preempted. Today, there are a multitude of alternatives to the major networks, what with the average viewer having a remote control and 62 channels from which to choose. Perhaps even more important has been the spread of video recorders. According to the U.S. Census, only 1 percent of homes owned a VCR in 1980, but by 1990 this device had nearly saturated the market and could be found in 69 percent of homes. VCRs freed viewers from the standard question of "What's on tonight?", allowing them to watch shows whenever they had the time. In sum, when regular programming is preempted on the major networks for a political event, most people now can turn either to the many alternatives offered via cable TV or to a videotape or DVD if they are not interested in politics.

Young people appear to be especially likely to make use of their television remote controls. In the 2002 Pew Research Center

Media Study, respondents were asked how many of the available channels they actually made use of. The mean for respondents under 30 years of age was 20 channels, compared to 15 for those between 30 and 64, and just 10 for senior citizens.[27] By switching to other programs when major political events are on, young adults have turned what used to be water-cooler shows into shows for older people. This transformation can be illustrated by an examination over time of viewing patterns of two institutionalized rituals in American presidential campaigns—political conventions and presidential debates.

Political party conventions used to receive more coverage on the major networks than the Summer Olympics. They dominated eight nights of prime-time programming every four years from 1952 to 1980. During this period, the standard practice for CBS, NBC, and ABC was to cover conventions from gavel-to-gavel, that is, whenever they were formally in session. Typically, each network provided about six hours a day of convention coverage.[28] Hence, when surveys asked whether people had seen the conventions in this period, almost everyone responded that he or she had. As can be seen in the data presented in Table 2.3, there was almost no relationship between age and having seen some convention coverage in 1972 and 1976. The extent that young people were slightly less likely to have tuned in to a convention was probably due to their having been outside taking advantage of the summer weather. By 2000 a whole generation of young adults had grown up with narrowcasting and without ever having experienced a suspenseful political convention. The result of these changes are clearly shown in the changing demographics of the convention audience, as senior citizens were almost twice as likely as people

TABLE 2.3

Percent Watching a Portion of Party Conventions by Age, 1972–2000

	18–29	30–44	45–64	65+	65+ / <30 RATIO
DEMOCRATIC CONVENTION					
1972	87	90	90	93	1.1 : 1
1976	70	80	90	92	1.3 : 1
2000	37	46	55	63	1.7 : 1
REPUBLICAN CONVENTION					
1972	70	82	79	79	1.1 : 1
1976	65	75	86	84	1.3 : 1
2000	35	44	53	62	1.8 : 1

Sources: 1972 Syracuse, NY, Survey; 1976 Erie, PA, and Los Angeles Surveys; 2000 National Annenberg Election Study.

aged 18 to 29 to report that they had watched some of the 2000 conventions.

It has been so long since anything newsworthy happened at an American political convention that college students reading this section today could justifiably ask whether the fact that their generation has largely tuned conventions out makes any difference. I would respond that their generation has missed out on tremendous opportunities for civic learning that previous generations benefited from. In addition to the marquee drama of watching the selection of the presidential and vice presidential nominees, viewers were also exposed to keynote speeches that identified the key principles of the parties, as well as to debates over the party platforms. Political conventions of the past thus provided a wide-open window into the workings of American party politics. This window has essentially been boarded up during the socialization of today's young adults.

In recent presidential campaigns, the only televised events with any sense of drama have been the presidential debates. Alan Schroeder summarizes the importance of these debates incisively:

> *In a fundamental way, American politics sorely needs these infusions of drama. One reason millions of citizens have disengaged from the process—young voters especially—is that they perceive electoral politics as boring. Annoying, largely uncreative campaign commercials, coupled with superficial press coverage and overly choreographed campaign events, have rendered presidential races needlessly dull. As the only stops on the campaign trail that cannot be totally foreordained, televised joint appearances offer insights into something the public too rarely gets to see: the human side of the candidates.*[29]

When Kennedy and Nixon met in four historic televised debates in 1960, they drew incredible ratings of between 58 and 61 on each occasion. Twenty years later, the one and only debate between Reagan and Carter generated the same level of audience interest, receiving a rating of 59. But with the end of the networks' captive hold on the TV audience, debate ratings have fallen substantially since 1980. In both 1996 and 2000, the presidential debates averaged an audience rating of just 28.[30]

As presidential debate ratings have declined, the representativeness of the viewing audience has naturally declined. When presidential debates were water-cooler events, young and senior citizens alike watched them. Such is the nature of water-cooler

TABLE 2.4
Percent Watching General Election Debates by Age, 1960–2000

	<30	30–44	45–64	65+	65+ / <30 RATIO
1960 KENNEDY–NIXON DEBATES	79	80	82	69	.9 : 1
1976 CARTER–FORD DEBATES	80	83	85	83	1.0 : 1
1980 REAGAN–CARTER DEBATE	62	69	73	76	1.2 : 1
1984 1ST REAGAN–MONDALE DEBATE	67	67	71	84	1.3 : 1
1984 2ND REAGAN–MONDALE DEBATE	59	65	76	88	1.5 : 1
1984 VP DEBATE	50	57	67	69	1.4 : 1
1996 1ST CLINTON–DOLE DEBATE	38	44	61	64	1.7 : 1
1996 2ND CLINTON–DOLE DEBATE	38	44	48	61	1.6 : 1
2000 1ST BUSH–GORE DEBATE	39	48	57	67	1.7 : 1
2000 2ND BUSH–GORE DEBATE	40	47	56	64	1.6 : 1
2000 3RD BUSH–GORE DEBATE	44	47	56	67	1.5 : 1
2000 VP DEBATE	22	30	41	53	2.4 : 1

Sources: 1960, 1976, and 1996 ANES; 1984 American National Election Study Continuous Monitoring Survey; 2000 National Annenberg Election Study.

shows. As Table 2.4 shows, it is clearly the younger generations who are responsible for the decline in the audience reach of presidential debates. In 2000, for example, two out of every three senior citizens interviewed said they had watched a particular presidential debate compared to only two out of five young adults. If Alan Schroeder is right in arguing that young Americans need to be convinced that politics is interesting, then it is unfortunate that they have become the least likely group to tune in to presidential debates in recent years.

On the other hand, it may well be that younger people are just more likely to consider presidential debates boring and hence deliberately don't tune in. A similar interpretation could be given for why young people are not watching TV news broadcasts. While this hypothesis is hard to disprove, I believe it is unlikely to be the case. Earlier generations were exposed to politics through news broadcasts and blockbuster political events that were hard to avoid in the era when three networks controlled 90 percent of the television audience. Many of these young adults learned through such television programming that politics was both important and interesting. Today's youth can hardly conclude that presidential debates and TV news broadcasts are boring if they have scarcely been exposed to them. And exposure seems to be the key problem in the narrowcasting age. Marshall McLuhan's famous saying about the media was that "the medium is the message."[31] In this case, the argument is essentially that the medium accounts for a lack of a message getting through to younger people. If the explanation for the trends displayed in this chapter stems from changes in the television medium, then similar patterns should be found in most other established democracies. Hence, comparative data provide a crucial test for this theory.

CAN SIMILAR PATTERNS BE FOUND IN OTHER ESTABLISHED DEMOCRACIES?

The early years of television news in other advanced industrialized countries were markedly different from those in the United States. Government-owned channels like the BBC dominated the airwaves in most other democracies. Given their government sponsorship, public service rather than profit was the driving force in the production of the news. To American eyes, the news on these channels was typically presented in a bland "just the facts" fashion. Living nearby the Canadian border during the late 1970s and early 1980s, I regularly got a chance to compare the *CBC News* to that of the American networks. As a graduate student interested in public policy, I found the Canadian news broadcasts to be highly informative, often dealing with complex issues in a way that seemed unimaginable on ABC, NBC, and CBS.

Indeed, what I observed from across the border formed a sharp contrast to the academic literature I was then reading about American TV news. The standard book at the time was Edward J. Epstein's *News from Nowhere*,[32] which summarized a year of his observing NBC's news department from inside the organization. Epstein found that in their pursuit of high ratings, news shows are tailored to a fairly low level of audience sophistication. To a large extent, American TV networks define news as what is entertaining to the average viewer. A dull and complicated story would have to be of enormous importance to get on the air; in contrast, relatively trivial stories can make the cut if they are interesting enough. As former *CBS News* reporter Bernard Goldberg writes, "In the United States of Entertainment there is no greater sin than to bore the audience."[33] While I don't mean to imply that Canadian TV news was boring (after all, I was regularly watching it), it was clear to me that entertainment was not their primary goal.

With a less entertaining style of presenting the news, it should not be surprising to find that news broadcasts in other democracies were not as widely watched as American network news at its peak of popularity in the late 1960s and early 1970s. A quick look at the comparative survey data bears out this expectation. The European

Communities Study (the precursor to the Eurobarometer) asked samples of five European nations how often they watched news broadcasts on television in 1970. The proportion saying they watched TV news every day was 61 percent in Germany, 59 percent in the Netherlands, 47 percent in France, 41 percent in Belgium, and 36 percent in Italy. In contrast, 72 percent of Americans interviewed in 1967 said they watched the TV news on a daily basis.

In spite of the lower audience levels for TV news in Western Europe in 1970, the age patterns for the five countries displayed in Table 2.5 are similar to those in the United States around that time in history. Even when American network TV news was incredibly popular, young adults were still the age group least likely to report

TABLE 2.5
Percent Watching the News on TV Every Day
in Five European Countries, 1970

	16–29	30–44	45–64	65+	DIFFERENCE BETWEEN 65+ AND 16–29	CORRELATION WITH AGE*
NETHERLANDS	45	64	68	78	+33	.18
FRANCE	31	46	55	57	+26	.17
BELGIUM	29	38	50	49	+20	.13
ITALY	30	33	41	38	+8	.00
WEST GERMANY	54	61	67	59	+5	.07

Question wording: "Do you watch news broadcasts on television: every day, several times a week, one or two times a week, less often, or never?"

*The correlations have been calculated by recoding the question responses as follows: every day = 100; several times a week = 50; one or two times a week = 25; less often = 10; never = 0.

Source: European Communities Study, 1970.

watching it every day. In part, this may stem from young adults' being less likely to be regularly at home during the evening. The fact that young people (defined as ages 16 to 29 in these surveys)[34] in each of the five European countries were the least likely to habitually watch the news would seem to support such an inference. On average, senior citizens in these countries were about 18 percent more likely than young people to say that they watched the news every day, a figure not notably higher than the 12 percent difference found at the same time in the United States.

European patterns of TV news viewing by age have changed dramatically since 1970. Just like in the United States, young Europeans are now much less likely than their elders to watch the news on television. Table 2.6 displays data from a 2000 Eurobarometer study that asked a very similar question to the one asked in 1970. For the five countries that were included in both studies, senior citizens in 2000 were 34 percent more likely to report watching the TV news on a daily basis than the youngest age group—nearly twice the comparable age gap found three decades earlier. And the average correlation between frequency of TV news viewing and age in these five countries was .25 in 2000 compared to .11 in 1970. Squaring these correlations in order to obtain the percentage of explained variance reveals that this represents a fivefold increase in the degree of variation in TV news viewing habits that can be explained by age.[35] Furthermore, due to the anomalous case of Italy, the average for these five countries is probably an underestimate for Europe as a whole. Expanding the analysis to all eleven established democracies included in the 2000 Eurobarometer study reveals that Italian young people were substantially more likely to watch TV news than young people

TABLE 2.6

Percent Watching the News on TV Every Day in 11 European
Countries, 2000

	16–29	30–44	45–64	65+	DIFFERENCE BETWEEN 65+ AND 16–29	CORRELATION BETWEEN TV NEWS WATCHING AND AGE
SWEDEN	45	65	81	93	+48	.38
IRELAND	45	66	75	87	+42	.34
WEST GERMANY	45	61	76	86	+41	.29
FRANCE	41	53	68	81	+40	.29
NETHERLANDS	56	76	83	96	+40	.28
DENMARK	53	71	85	92	+39	.34
AUSTRIA	45	60	73	83	+38	.31
BELGIUM	44	64	76	81	+37	.29
GREAT BRITAIN	56	69	82	91	+35	.29
FINLAND	66	78	86	95	+29	.21
ITALY	76	80	90	87	+11	.11

Question wording: "About how often do you watch the news on television: every day, several times a week, one or two times a week, less often, or never?"

Source: November–December 2000 Eurobarometer.

elsewhere in Western Europe. Excluding Italy, the average correlation between age and TV news viewing in 2000 was .30 in the other ten countries.[36]

Overall, a higher percentage of Europeans said they were watching TV news every day in 2000 than in 1970. It should be noted that the question asked in both studies was a relatively broad one. Respondents could have been thinking of cable news channels as well as national broadcast news. The addition of cable news to the news menu by 2000 probably accounts for why Europeans reported more frequent news viewing in the latter period. But even with cable news included in the picture, the data show a marked bias toward an older audience for television news in Europe. As the number of channels that Europeans have to choose from has increased, younger people have been the ones least likely to choose the news.

Of course, TV news involves all sorts of subjects, and it is not necessarily the case that viewers are watching political stories. A more specific test of the narrowcasting argument can be made by looking at viewing rates of specific political events. Leadership debates prior to a general election are the one common type of political event that has been held in a number of established democracies over the past 40 years. As in the United States, these debates have provided citizens with excellent opportunities to size up and compare those who aspire to their nation's highest political office. And as has been the case with U.S. presidential debates, these televised discussions have often provided the most dramatic moments of the campaign. For example, when Canadian Liberal Leader John Turner charged in a 1988 debate that Prime Minister Brian Mulroney had sold out Canada by signing the free trade deal with the United States, he scored perhaps the biggest point of the campaign. Similarly, a key event in the 2004 Australian election occurred when Labor Leader Mark Latham accused Prime Minister John Howard during their one televised debate of ignoring nearby national security concerns while sending military resources to Iraq.[37]

Both these recent memorable leadership debates were far more likely to be seen by older voters than younger ones. As Table 2.7 shows, Canadian senior citizens were 1.8 times more

TABLE 2.7
Percent Watching Party Leader Debates in Various Countries

	<30	30–44	45–64	65+	65+ / <30 RATIO
SWEDEN 1964**	66	68	70	64	1.0 : 1
NORWAY 1965*	48	56	59	62	1.3 : 1
NORWAY 1969*	55	58	65	70	1.3 : 1
CANADA 1968*	57	67	65	56	1.0 : 1
CANADA 1979*	46	51	55	58	1.3 : 1
CANADA 1984**	60	63	73	80	1.3 : 1
CANADA 1988*	42	50	64	72	1.8 : 1
CANADA 1993**	39	50	59	74	1.9 : 1
CANADA 1997**	35	46	56	66	1.9 : 1
CANADA 2000**	28	47	49	67	2.4 : 1
CANADA 2004**	37	42	55	64	1.7 : 1
GERMANY 1972**	79	90	86	73	.9 : 1
GERMANY 1976*	74	77	78	72	1.0 : 1
GERMANY 2002 #1	41	51	57	54	1.3 : 1
GERMANY 2002 #2	38	49	62	66	1.7 : 1
NETHERLANDS 1982*	43	53	61	66	1.5 : 1
NETHERLANDS 1986*	54	53	58	71	1.3 : 1
NETHERLANDS 1989*	38	44	56	67	1.8 : 1
NETHERLANDS 1994*	42	59	53	65	1.5 : 1
NETHERLANDS 1998**	42	43	49	63	1.5 : 1
FRANCE 1988*	60	70	79	85	1.4 : 1
NEW ZEALAND 2002**	55	63	73	81	1.5 : 1
AUSTRALIA 1990*	37	53	62	73	2.0 : 1
AUSTRALIA 1993**	54	66	75	81	1.5 : 1

(Continued)

TABLE 2.7 (Continued)

	<30	30–44	45–64	65+	65+ / <30 RATIO
AUSTRALIA 1996**	45	50	63	73	1.6 : 1
AUSTRALIA 1998*	25	33	47	67	2.7 : 1
AUSTRALIA 2001*	24	32	43	60	2.5 : 1
AUSTRALIA 2004*	25	28	32	53	2.1 : 1

*Survey asked about only one debate.
**Survey asked about multiple debates.

Source: National election studies for countries and years shown.

likely than those under the age of 30 to say they had watched the 1988 leadership debate. In contrast, 20 years earlier in Canada there was no relationship between age and debate viewing. The data from eight Canadian election studies from 1968 to 2004 clearly show that as choices on television have proliferated, young people have opted out of watching political debates.

Although the time series for Australian debates is too limited to draw conclusions about changes over time, it is clear that young Australians have not been particularly inclined to watch recent debates. The 2004 Australian debate was viewed by 53 percent of seniors, as compared to just 25 percent of Australians between the ages of 18 and 29. This debate faced stiff competition in its time slot from *Australian Idol*, a popular show following the format of *American Idol* in the United States. Overall, the rating for *Australian Idol* was 40 percent higher than that for the so-called "great debate." This came as no surprise to Australia's Treasurer Peter Costello, who told the Australian Associated Press that he had predicted that entertainment would trump politics in the ratings. Costello added that "I checked with my kids at home whether they were watching the debate or *Australian Idol* and Idol was winning hands down. I think a lot of people would have turned it on and had a look to see how it was going and then they'd start wavering with the finger on the remote control."[38] Although the children of the nation's treasurer were not yet old enough to vote, they were nevertheless typical of young Australian adults.

These Canadian and Australian examples are indicative of a major change in viewing patterns for leadership debates. In order to summarize the age viewing patterns, the ratio of old to young debate viewers is calculated in Table 2.7 for 28 separate election studies from eight different countries. In the 1960s and 1970s, this ratio averaged 1.1 to 1, meaning that senior citizens were only slightly more likely than young adults to tune in to a debate. By the 1980s, this ratio had changed to 1.5 to 1, and in the 1990s and early twenty-first century, it was 1.9 to 1. In sum, these debates are no longer shared national experiences. As in the United States, such programming appeals primarily to older people. Consequently, the concerns of young adults are not likely to be major foci of these important public policy forums.

CONCLUSION: CAN SOFT NEWS SAVE THE DAY?

For simple economic reasons, commercial television news producers would not be operating rationally if they were to ignore young adults completely. As economist James T. Hamilton points out in his book *All the News That's Fit to Sell*, two fundamental considerations for news producers are "Who cares about a particular piece of information?" and "What are others willing to pay to reach them?"[39] The results of this chapter would certainly not lead news producers to focus on young adults as the answer to Hamilton's first question. But the answer to the second question should give them some incentive to try to shape news programs in a way to attract more young people. For as Hamilton also points out, advertisers will often pay top dollar to reach young adult viewers because their purchasing decisions are less likely to be determined by brand-name loyalties.[40] Thus, if young adults aren't tuning in to traditional news broadcasts, the marketplace provides special incentives for news producers to package the news in alternative ways that might appeal to young people.

One way that the news business has adapted to the shrinking market for conventional news broadcasts has been to produce news shows designed primarily for the purpose of entertainment rather than for providing information. This TV genre has come to be known as "soft news." Some examples of soft news shows on American television include *Dateline, Inside Edition,* and *Extra.* Although these shows are not intended to serve the public interest by enlightening viewers about the details of current events, Matthew Baum argues that under the right circumstances, they can have just that effect. He maintains that such shows have the potential to expose a broader segment of the public to "information about select high-profile political issues, including foreign policy crises, that involve scandal, violence, heroism, or other forms of sensational human drama."[41] With all sorts of entertainment shows covering a major political crisis in a different fashion than straight news shows, Baum concludes that it is more difficult than ever before to avoid exposure to the most dramatic and incredible news stories of the day. His impressive data analysis shows that the sorts of people who typically tune out politics have clearly learned a good deal about recent foreign policy crises from viewing soft news programs. The result has been a broader public knowledge of major foreign policy crises in the narrowcasting environment than in the old broadcasting era.

Baum's findings about soft news can conceivably be applied to the questions raised by this chapter. Young adults may not be paying attention to hard news shows or traditional political events, but they do like to be entertained. Thus, if soft news shows can provide entertaining coverage of political events, then they may well have the potential to save the day by making young people aware of at least some aspects of current events.

One has to be skeptical, however, of whether very many political stories will ever receive this sort of entertainment news coverage. Aside from the wars, foreign crises, and scandals that Baum examines, there is much reason to doubt whether political events ever penetrate into young people's consciousness through this sort of viewing osmosis. In short, there is good reason to suspect that the cases Baum examines are the exception rather than the rule. The next chapter attempts to establish what the norm is for political stories and how it has changed over the last few decades.

CHAPTER 3

Don't Ask Anyone Under 30

When successive generations largely fail to get into the twin habits of reading a newspaper and watching TV news, there are bound to be political consequences. Important political events often fall on deaf ears among many young people today. Such was not the case when many young people were active newspaper readers and frequently watched political coverage on TV. Now that they largely do neither of these activities, it is to be expected that older people will follow political news stories much more closely than younger people will.

When I was growing up, a common political saying was "Don't trust anyone over 30," reflecting the fact that many young people were challenging the political establishment. Today when it comes to political news stories, one could reasonably say, "Don't ask anyone under 30," as chances are good that he or she won't have heard of these stories. Young adults today can hardly challenge the establishment if they don't have a basic grasp of what is going on in the political world.

In the first part of this chapter, we will examine data on whether people of different age groups say they have followed major political events. This is important in and of itself, because if younger people aren't following what's going on in politics, they are at a sharp disadvantage in being able to direct how politicians deal with the issues of the day. Furthermore, if young people are tuned out from current events, then one of the results should be that they won't know as much about politics as their elders—a topic that will be examined in the second part of this chapter.

HAVE YOUNG PEOPLE BECOME LESS LIKELY TO FOLLOW POLITICAL EVENTS?

From time to time, the U.S. National Election Studies have asked respondents for their opinions about current events. Recognizing that not everyone will be familiar with even the most highly publicized news stories, these studies have typically first asked a filter question to ascertain whether people were aware of them. For example, in 1968 respondents were asked, "Did you happen to hear anything about what went on between the police and the demonstrators in Chicago at the Democratic Convention?" Those who replied affirmatively were then asked whether the police had used too much force or not. The principal investigators at the time were really interested in the responses to the latter question, but for the purposes of this chapter, we are interested only in the first question, that is, whether or not people followed what happened. All told, I was able to locate such questions on ten major news stories that were asked about during election years from 1948 and 2004. If recent generations have not followed current events due to the ease with which they can tune out news in the narrowcasting age, then we should find a change in attention patterns by age from the broadcasting to the narrowcasting eras. The data displayed in Table 3.1 provide supporting evidence for this theory.

TABLE 3.1

Percent Following Major Events in Election
Years by Age, 1948–2004

	<30	30–44	45–64	65+	DIFFERENCE BETWEEN 65+ AND <30
HEARD SOMETHING ABOUT THE TAFT–HARTLEY ACT, 1948*	58	57	58	52	−6
HEARD ABOUT THE CIVIL RIGHTS BILL, 1964	77	80	72	66	−11
HEARD DISCUSSION OF HOW THE ELECTORAL COLLEGE SYSTEM MIGHT AFFECT THE CHOICE OF THE NEW PRESIDENT BECAUSE OF WALLACE BEING IN THE RACE, 1968	52	55	54	38	−14
HEARD ABOUT WHAT WENT ON BETWEEN THE POLICE AND THE DEMONSTRATORS IN CHICAGO AT THE DEMOCRATIC CONVENTION, 1968	90	89	89	82	−8
REMEMBERED SOMETHING ABOUT THE EAGLETON CONTROVERSY, 1972	74	78	74	60	−14
HEARD ENOUGH ABOUT WHAT IS GOING ON IN SOUTH AFRICA TO HAVE AN OPINION ABOUT WHAT U.S. POLICY SHOULD BE, 1988	30	46	43	40	+10

(Continued)

TABLE 3.1 (Continued)

	<30	30–44	45–64	65+	DIFFERENCE BETWEEN 65+ AND <30
HEARD A LOT ABOUT THE CHANGES TAKING PLACE IN THE SOVIET UNION AND EASTERN EUROPE, 1990	27	37	46	53	+26
HEARD A LOT OR SOME ABOUT THE CHANGES TAKING PLACE IN THE SOVIET UNION AND EASTERN EUROPE, 1990	77	83	83	85	+8
HEARD ABOUT THE PROBLEMS IN THE SAVINGS AND LOAN BUSINESS, 1990	55	75	79	72	+17
HEARD ABOUT U.S. REPRESENTATIVES WRITING CHECKS WHEN THEY DIDN'T HAVE ENOUGH MONEY TO COVER THEM IN THEIR HOUSE BANK ACCOUNT, 1992	82	89	92	86	+4
HEARD A LOT ABOUT THE U.S. PLANNING TO HAND OVER CIVILIAN AUTHORITY TO IRAQI LEADERS, 2004	23	41	52	50	+27
HEARD A LOT OR A LITTLE ABOUT THE U.S. PLANNING TO HAND OVER CIVILIAN AUTHORITY TO IRAQI LEADERS, 2004	67	83	89	90	+23

*In 1948 the age categories were as follows: 21–34, 35–44, 45–64, 65+.

Sources: U.S. National Election Studies, 1948–1992; Pew Center June 2004 Study.

During the broadcast era, younger people were actually *more likely* to say they had heard of major news stories of the election season than senior citizens were. The Taft–Hartley Act constraining the practices of labor unions was one of the most hotly debated matters of the 1948 campaign, with Democrats regularly referring to it as the "slave labor act." When asked about this bill during the 1948 National Election Study, senior citizens were least likely to report having heard something about it. Similarly, 16 years later when the 1964 Civil Rights Act was one of the top news stories of the day, the elderly expressed the lowest degree of awareness of it. As part of the backlash against the civil rights movement, George Wallace of Alabama mounted a significant independent candidacy for president in 1968. Because of Wallace's regional base in the deep South, the media focused on the very real possibility that there might not be a majority winner in the electoral college vote. In the 1968 National Election Study, respondents under 30 were about a third more likely than senior citizens to say they had heard discussion about this prospect. Similarly, younger people in the same study were the most likely to say they had heard about the violence at the Democratic Convention in Chicago—hardly a surprising finding given that the violence was directed at young demonstrators. Four years later, one of the big news stories of the campaign involved the removal of Senator Eagleton from the Democratic ticket after stories emerged concerning his past treatment for clinical depression. When respondents were asked whether they remembered anything about the Eagleton controversy, once again we find a pattern of young people being more aware of a big election news story than the elderly.

Unfortunately, there were no specific questions about current events in the election surveys conducted between 1972 and 1988. During this period, the media environment changed markedly, as did the age pattern in following current events. In 1988, young people were substantially less likely than other age groups to have heard about the controversy regarding the South African racial apartheid policy. This finding is particularly noteworthy in light of the fact that opposition to apartheid in South Africa was a much-talked-about cause on college campuses throughout the 1980s. Two years later, earthshaking events were taking place throughout Eastern Europe, as the domino theory ended up applying to European communism. Though it was young people who were at the forefront of demonstrations in places such as East Berlin, Prague, and Bucharest, young Americans were the least likely to have heard about the revolutions in Eastern Europe. In this case, respondents were asked whether they had heard a lot or just some about these changes. Senior citizens were roughly twice as likely as people under 30 years of age to say that they had heard a lot about them. Furthermore, it was not just foreign events that young respondents in 1990 were unaware of. On the domestic side, young people were also the least likely to have heard about the exorbitant cost of government bailouts for the troubled savings and loan industry, which was then at the forefront of the news. Two years later, the under-30 group was slightly less likely than older people to have heard about the scandal regarding bad check writing among members of the House of Representatives. And most recently, in June 2004 a Pew Research Center survey found that young people were not following to nearly the same degree as older people the plan to hand over civilian authority to Iraqi leaders.

In sum, whereas older people used to be the least likely to follow major news stories of election years, the pattern has now been sharply reversed. Today, the older someone is, the more likely he or she is to be aware of a top news story. Of course, this pattern might be different for less prominent news stories that occur out of the spotlight of a national election. Matthew Baum's work on soft news and foreign policy might lead us to expect that young people would be relatively more aware of such issues today than they were several decades ago. A comparison of data from a 1974 survey conducted by the Chicago Council on Foreign Relations and some recent Pew Research Center polls highlights one telling test of this hypothesis.

As can be seen from Table 3.2, there was only a slight relationship between age and one's following foreign news stories in December 1974. This survey on American foreign policy and public opinion asked people how closely they had followed 11 of the most prominent foreign news stories of the year. Overall, the survey found that relatively few Americans paid very close attention to international relations matters. For the typical event asked about in late 1974, just 19 percent said they followed the news about it "very closely," compared to 47 percent who said "not very closely." In the shorthand index employed in Table 3.2, this registers as an index value of −28, as the percentage who did not follow the event is subtracted from the percentage that followed it very closely. Reading across the various rows, one can see that the relationship between age and following foreign news events was generally quite minimal in 1974. In three cases (the World Food Conference, Vietnam, and the Cyprus War), young people were actually the most likely to follow the news. In seven cases, older people were somewhat more likely to follow foreign policy stories, and in the case of problems in the Middle East, the correlation with age was nonexistent at .00. Overall, the average correlation between age and the 11 items that were asked about was a mere .03.

Twenty-eight years later, the pattern had changed markedly, with attention to foreign news increasing substantially with a respondent's age. The Pew Research Center now regularly asks

TABLE 3.2

Degree to Which People of Different Ages Followed Foreign
News Stories in 1974 [entries = % responding
very closely − % responding not very closely]

	18–29	30–49	50–64	65+	CORRELATION WITH AGE
WORLD FOOD CONFERENCE	+3	−4	−4	−13	−.05
WHAT'S HAPPENING IN VIETNAM THESE DAYS	−30	−41	−41	−36	−.04
CYPRUS WAR	−30	−38	−29	−39	−.02
PROBLEMS IN THE MIDDLE EAST	−2	+4	+5	−9	.00
KISSINGER'S TRIP TO CHINA	−4	−6	−2	0	.02
ARAFAT'S VISIT TO THE UN	−31	−30	−19	−28	.04
CONGRESSIONAL DEBATES ON FOREIGN DEFENSE SPENDING	−32	−30	−25	−28	.04
CONGRESSIONAL DEBATES ON FOREIGN AID	−42	−36	−26	−35	.06
ELECTIONS IN GREAT BRITAIN	−71	−72	−55	−62	.08
DISCUSSIONS ABOUT THE U.S. RECOGNIZING CUBA	−32	−30	−12	−23	.09
FORD-BREZHNEV SUMMIT MEETING	−43	−37	−15	−20	.14
AVERAGE	−29	−29	−20	−26	.03

Question wording: "How closely would you say you personally have followed news about the following events—very closely, somewhat closely, or not very closely?"

Source: Chicago Council on Foreign Relations Survey conducted by Harris, December 6–14, 1974.

their survey respondents how closely they have followed the biggest news stories of the past month. These stories primarily involve domestic concerns, but in December 2002 and January 2003, they focused mostly on foreign affairs, asking about nine separate foreign stories. Overall, the American public followed these stories more closely than they had followed the major foreign stories of 1974. Thirty-one percent said that they followed the news about the typical recent foreign policy story "very closely" compared to 19 percent in 1974, and the average percentage of people not following such stories declined from 47 to 36 percent. This results in an attention index value of −5 for 2002–2003, as compared to −28 in 1974. Such an increase in attention to foreign events is consistent with Baum's findings. But the data by age group shown in Table 3.3 presents a new twist. Among adults under the age of 30, the typical level of attention paid to foreign events was nearly identical in the two eras. By contrast, the average increase in attention was 22 points for the 30 to 49 age group, 31 points for the 50- to 64-year-olds, and 34 points for senior citizens. The end result is that the average correlation between age and following foreign news was .17 for the 2002–2003 period as compared to just .03 in 1974. Granted, these were different stories, and in the recent era, America considered itself at war whereas in the earlier period it had not. Nevertheless, there is one item that is quite similar in both periods—the Middle East—for which the correlation with age increased from .00 to .18.

One might think that young people need some substantial life experiences in order to become aware of how much things that happen far away from home in places like the Middle East may affect one's own life. But in the recent era of globalization, this

TABLE 3.3

Degree to Which People of Different Ages Followed Foreign News Stories in 2002–2003 [entries = % responding very closely − % responding not too closely/not at all closely]

	18–29	30–49	50–64	65+	CORRELATION WITH AGE
DEBATE OVER THE POSSIBILITY THAT THE U.S. WILL TAKE MILITARY ACTION IN IRAQ	+15	+39	+46	+38	.12
THE WORK OF UN WEAPONS INSPECTORS IN IRAQ (DEC. 2002)	−12	+14	+25	+15	.12
THE WORK OF UN WEAPONS INSPECTORS IN IRAQ (JAN. 2003)	−11	+6	+25	+25	.14
TERRORIST ATTACKS IN KENYA AGAINST ISRAELI CITIZENS	−49	−21	−4	−14	.17
DEBATE OVER THE POSSIBILITY THAT THE U.S. WILL TAKE MILITARY ACTION IN IRAQ	+26	+33	+57	+62	.17
CONTINUED VIOLENCE IN THE MIDDLE EAST BETWEEN THE PALESTINIANS AND THE ISRAELIS	−32	−6	+14	+6	.18
THE LARGE OIL SPILL POLLUTING THE COAST OF SPAIN	−67	−42	−26	−23	.20
NORTH KOREA'S NUCLEAR WEAPONS PROGRAM	−29	−5	+25	+20	.21
POLITICAL INSTABILITY IN VENEZUELA	−87	−79	−66	−54	.25
AVERAGE	−27	−7	+11	+8	.17

Question wording: "Now I will read a list of some things that have been in the news this past month. As I read each item, tell me if you happened to follow this news story very closely, fairly closely, not too closely, or not at all closely."

Source: Pew Research Center surveys, December 2002 & January 2003.

seems less likely to be the case than ever before, especially considering how the Internet has made it is easier than ever to obtain news about foreign events. Furthermore, one would think that the prospect of an imminent war with Iraq would make young people in the later period more likely—not less—to follow international relations, given that their generation would be the one called upon to do most of the fighting.

What News Stories Did Young People Follow in 2004?

If young people are paying less attention to wars that may well involve their age group, one must wonder what news stories, if any, they are particularly attentive to. In May 2004 the Pew Research Center asked a random sample of over five thousand Americans how much they followed 14 separate types of news stories. Out of all these news categories, there were only four that young people followed more closely than older people: 1) entertainment; 2) sports; 3) science and technology; and 4) culture and the arts. Of these four, only in the case of entertainment was the tendency for young people to follow the news more closely as strong as the tendency for older people to follow political news more closely. As David Mindich writes, the biggest change in the media environment in recent decades has been "the entertainment revolution, allowing young people basically unlimited entertainment options 24 hours a day."[42] Based on Mindich's in-depth conversations with numerous young people, he asserts that "If we want to understand why many young people don't follow the news, we need to understand the lure of entertainment."[43]

Young Americans' preference for entertainment over politics is clearly illustrated by an analysis of the Pew Research Center's data on what major news stories people paid attention to throughout 2004. During the course of the entire year, these studies asked about all sorts of news stories that were given prominent coverage in the media. Table 3.4 summarizes generational differences in attention paid to the 36 stories the Pew Research Center asked about from January through September 2004. The three news stories that young adults paid more attention to than senior citizens did were all entertainment stories—the Summer Olympics and the release of two controversial movies. Similarly, the five stories that young people were almost as likely to follow as older people were of the sort that one might see covered on soft news shows such as *Extra* or *Dateline*. Janet Jackson's "wardrobe malfunction" at the Super Bowl halftime show was probably the most-talked-about entertainment story of the year; the landing on Mars provided spectacular photos that were perfect for soft news shows; and the high price of gasoline was a story that anyone with a car would be interested in. Although the 9/11 Commission hearings and the abuse of Iraqi prisoners at Abu Ghraib were political stories, each had sensationalistic aspects to them that could be spun so as to provide entertainment.

In contrast, the stories that were followed far more closely by the elderly were frequently of the "Inside the Beltway" political variety. In other words, they were the sorts of stories that would receive time on shows that provide in-depth discussion of political events, such as *Washington Week in Review* on PBS or *Capital Gang* on CNN. For example, stories like Richard Clarke's criticism of the Bush administration's handling of terrorist threats and

TABLE 3.4

Extent to Which Adults Under 30 Followed 2004 News Stories Compared to Senior Citizens

Stories Young Adults Paid More Attention to than Seniors

Summer Olympics in Athens—Aug. and Sept.
Release of movie *Fahrenheit 9/11*—July
Release of movie *The Passion of the Christ*—March

Stories Young Adults Paid Slightly Less Attention to than Seniors

9/11 Commission Hearings—April
Janet Jackson Super Bowl show—Feb.
High price of gasoline—asked in five monthly surveys
Abuse of Iraqi prisoners—June
NASA landing spacecraft on Mars—Jan.

Stories Young Adults Paid Substantially Less Attention to than Seniors

Bill Clinton's book—July
Democratic Convention—Aug.
Republican Convention—Sept.
Current situation in Iraq—asked in seven monthly surveys
Gay marriage debate—Feb. & March
Terrorist bombings in Spain—March
Ethnic violence in Sudan—July
2004 presidential election—asked in seven monthly surveys
Unrest in Haiti—March
Death of Ronald Reagan—June
Reports of Mad Cow Disease—Jan.
Saddam Hussein's court appearance—July
Code Orange alert—Jan. & Aug.
Hurricanes in the southeast—Sept.
Transfer of power in Iraq—July

Stories Young Adults Paid Far Less Attention to than Seniors

Ads by the Swift Boat Veterans—Sept.
Reports that Libya will end its weapons program—Jan.
No WMD found in Iraq—Feb.
Conviction of Martha Stewart—March
Democratic vice presidential nomination—July
Bill Clinton's heart surgery—Sept.
Killing of Russian schoolchildren—Sept.
Pres. Bush's National Guard service—Feb. & Sept.

(Continued)

TABLE 3.4 (Continued)

Richard Clarke's criticism of Bush administration—April
Ricin found in Senate office building—Feb.
Recent attacks on civilians and troops in Iraq—April
Reports about the U.S. economy—Jan. & Sept.
Earthquake in Iran—Jan.

Note: For each question, an attention index was calculated for those under 30 years of age and those over 65. The index value for young adults was then subtracted from the index value for senior citizens. The categories above were determined as follows: slightly less attention = difference of 20 points or fewer; substantially less attention = difference of between 21 and 40 points; far less attention = difference of over 40 points. Items within each category are ordered from those with the lowest index difference to those with the highest.

Source: 2004 Pew Research Center surveys.

the ads by the Swift Boat Veterans criticizing Senator John Kerry's service in Vietnam provided lively discussion for such shows. The fact that older people were more attentive to such specific campaign stories certainly demonstrates that they were following the day-to-day events of the 2004 campaign more closely than were younger people.

However, if much of what young people are missing out on are stories that could be labeled under the "Inside the Beltway" rubric, then perhaps there are relatively few consequences of the changing age demographics for political news. Though it might be crucial to have heard about the Swift Boat ads in order to understand how the 2004 campaign turned out, it wasn't necessary to know about them in order to be an informed voter. In other words, are young people really learning less of what they really need to know?

I would argue that the lack of attention young adults currently pay to mainstream media has led them to miss out on many highly consequential political stories. It should be noted that two of the 2004 stories that young adults paid relatively little attention to compared to the elderly were: 1) reports that weapons of mass destruction had not been found in Iraq; and 2) reports about the condition of the U.S. economy. Surely exposure to both these stories would have helped citizens make a well-informed judgment concerning how well President Bush had performed in his first term.

The next section addresses the question of whether today's young adults are in fact less informed about politics due to their not reading newspapers, not watching TV news, and not following political stories to the same degree as previous generations of young people.

IS THIS THE LEAST POLITICALLY KNOWLEDGEABLE GENERATION OF AMERICAN YOUTH EVER?

Since the advent of academic survey research in the 1940s, probably the most dramatic sociological development has been the tremendous increase in public levels of formal education. This steady rise in education levels has been driven by the replacement of cohorts who averaged less than 10 years of education by new generations who have averaged over 13 years of schooling.[44] If one had asked scholars in the 1940s what consequences could be expected from rising education levels, one common answer would surely have been that political knowledge would increase. In the 1948 National Election Study, the correlation between education and the measure that was developed for political knowledge was .31. Fifty-six years later in 2004 the correlation between the same two variables was quite similar at .37. Given this relatively constant relationship between political knowledge and education, it is quite logical to expect that a better-educated population should be a more politically knowledgeable one. However, Delli Carpini and Keeter's comprehensive work on the subject entitled *What Americans Know About Politics and Why It Matters* finds that this has not been the case.[45] They postulate that a general decline in political engagement has offset the positive impact of rising education levels.

The findings of this book provide a more detailed explanation as to why today's well-educated young Americans have not ushered in a new age of a more politically informed public. More access to higher education has provided recent generations with the ability to learn more about politics than their grandparents were able to. But just because the potential is there doesn't mean that someone will use it. Without reading a daily newspaper, watching the TV news, or otherwise following current events, even the best-educated people will probably not pick up much knowledge about the political world. A lack of basic educational skills might make it difficult for someone to absorb political information, but even the most advanced educational skills will not help if one is not exposed to current affairs through the news.

Given their relative lack of exposure to political news and current events, young people should be falling more and more behind their elders in terms of political knowledge despite their relatively high levels of educational achievement. Table 3.5 provides American National Election Studies data from over half a century to support this hypothesis. In 18 different election studies, a variety of factual questions about politics were posed to respondents, such as, "Do you happen to know: what position this person holds? which party now has the most members in the Senate? who

TABLE 3.5

Changing Political Knowledge/Age Relationship in United States
[entries = average % correct on factual questions]

	<30	30–44	45–64	65+	CORRELATION BETWEEN AGE AND KNOWLEDGE, CONTROLLING FOR EDUCATION
1948*	44	48	46	33	.03
1960	55	63	61	53	.06
1964	66	72	68	61	.06
1966	49	48	49	40	.09
1968	61	60	61	52	.03
1972	51	54	52	47	.11
1976	53	64	64	57	.20
1980	38	46	45	42	.15
1984	38	45	50	43	.21
1986	28	39	40	35	.21
1988	32	48	51	48	.30
1990	26	35	37	36	.27
1992	28	36	40	38	.26
1994	39	55	57	57	.26
1996	57	65	67	65	.16
1998	47	52	60	58	.22
2000	34	44	52	50	.28
2004	36	47	52	55	.27

*In 1948 the age categories were as follows: 21–34, 35–44, 45–64, 65+.

Note: See the Appendix to Chapter 3 for a list of questions employed in each year.

Source: American National Election Studies.

nominates federal judges?,", etc. With the exception of the 1948 questions, it is a simple matter to code the responses into variables measuring whether the correct factual answer was provided or not and to calculate the percentage of correct answers within each age group. In 1948, respondents were asked a set of five questions about what was going on in the Cold War, and interviewers were responsible for classifying each person's level of information into four categories—none, low, medium, or high. These four categories were recoded from 0 to 100, and then means were calculated for each age group. Thus, in each case the entries in Table 3.5 range from 0, representing the least political knowledge, to 100, representing the most. Because the questions were different in every year, one cannot infer anything about whether overall political knowledge went up or down each year. All that these data can tell us is whether the relationship between age and political knowledge has changed, which indeed it has.

From 1948 through 1972, the elderly were consistently the least politically knowledgeable age group. The relative lack of political information among the elderly during this period was probably due to their rather low levels of formal education. For example, three out of five senior citizens in 1960 reported having just a grade school education (i.e., eight years or less of schooling). Thus, in order to understand the relationship between age and political knowledge, it is necessary to control for education. A simple way to accomplish this is to calculate a correlation that holds the level of education constant (in technical parlance, a "partial correlation"). These correlations are displayed in the far-right-hand column of Table 3.5. As expected, once the low levels of formal education among the elderly during this period are taken into account, a slight tendency is found for political knowledge to increase with age.

Since 1976, young adults have consistently scored the lowest in terms of answering these factual questions. At first, young adults were only slightly below other age groups, but this gap has widened considerably in recent years. In 2004, for example, senior citizens knew the correct answer 55 percent of the time, whereas young adults responded with the right answer just 36 percent of the time. With so much data over so many years, the most effective way of summarizing the trend is to average out the correlations, controlling for education by decade. These averages nicely illustrate how the political knowledge gap between young and old has accelerated over time:

1948 = .03
1960s = .06
1970s = .16
1980s = .22
1990s = .23
2000s = .28

Furthermore, a more detailed analysis of the recent data shows that it is not just one or two items that cause young people to score lower on the index. People under 30 have consistently scored lower than other age groups on each and every factual question in recent surveys. Regardless of whether the question concerned basic civics facts, identification of current political leaders, information about the presidential candidates, or knowledge of partisan control of the Congress, the result was the same: young people were clearly less well-informed than the elderly. The title of this chapter—"Don't

Ask Anyone Under 30"—can thus be applied not only to current political events but also to general political knowledge in the United States.

ARE YOUNG PEOPLE IN OTHER DEMOCRACIES SIMILARLY CLUELESS ABOUT POLITICS?

Young people in the United States are far from unique in not following public affairs and possessing relatively less knowledge of politics compared to older people. These same patterns can be found throughout the established democratic world in recent years. Although relevant data are not as plentiful for other democracies over time, what early data are available show that this has not always been the case.

Cross-national studies of political behavior typically focus on universal questions that will be relevant across a variety of different countries, thereby making it impossible to replicate the American analysis regarding age patterns for following current events. Thus, we will have to rely on general questions that have been asked concerning how frequently citizens follow political affairs. The authors of the classic 1959–1960 Civic Culture Study considered following politics on a regular basis to be an integral part of what the authors termed "the self-confident citizen" who feels capable of political participation.[46] Table 3.6 displays the age patterns for how often people said they followed accounts of political and governmental affairs in the Civic Culture Study. The summary figures indicate that there was only a slight

TABLE 3.6

Degree of Following Accounts of Political and Governmental Affairs by Age, Circa 1960 [entries = % responding regularly − % responding never]

	18–30	31–40	41–60	61+	CORRELATION WITH AGE
USA	−4	+6	+13	+13	.11
UK	−19	−12	−3	−9	.08
GERMANY	−2	+19	+9	+14	.04
ITALY	−54	−43	−55	−59	−.03

Question wording: "Do you follow the accounts of political and governmental affairs—would you say you follow them regularly, from time to time, or never?"

Source: 1959–1960 Civic Culture Study.

tendency for older people to follow politics more regularly in the United States, the United Kingdom, and Germany, with this pattern being reversed in Italy.

The 1959 data from Italy shed much light on the anomalous Italian patterns that were found in the previous two chapters. Unlike the case in other established democracies, recent Italian survey data show relatively little in the way of generational differences in reading newspapers and watching TV news. A close examination of how Italy compares to the rest of Western Europe reveals that what is exceptional is how infrequently older Italians currently read newspapers and watch TV news compared to senior citizens in other established democracies. The Italian 1959 data displayed in Table 3.6 put the experience of today's elderly Italians into perspective. At that point in time, Italians fell far below Americans, British, and Germans in terms of levels of following politics. An incredible 63 percent of all Italians interviewed in 1959 said they *never* followed accounts of political and governmental affairs. Such findings led Almond and Verba to call Italy "an alienated political culture" in which "Italians tend to look upon government and politics as unpredictable and threatening forces, and not as social institutions amenable to their influence."[47] According to the socialization framework of this book, having grown up in such an environment is bound to have long-term consequences. In most established democracies, today's senior citizens came of age at a time when most people were attentive to political news, and hence have maintained this habit throughout their lifetimes. However, this was not the case in Italy, and the legacy of the 1950s can be seen in the data to this day among Italian senior citizens.

In most countries, the different socialization experiences of young and old have resulted by the beginning of the twenty-first century in a wide generation gap in the likelihood of following politics. Table 3.7 presents some data from the most recent World Values Study, conducted between 1999 and 2001, that illustrate this point very nicely. As with the wording of the question from the Civic Culture Study, the World Values Study asked a general question concerning how often people followed politics. In every one of the 14 established democracies where this question was asked, younger people reported paying significantly less attention to political news. As shown in the far-right-hand column, the correlation between age and following politics ranged from a low of .13 in Italy to a high of .40 in Japan, with an average of .26. In simple terms that demonstrate the basic point, 65 percent of senior citizens in the typical established democracy said that

TABLE 3.7

Percent Who Say They Follow Politics in the News Every Day in Established Democracies by Age, Circa 2000

	18–29	30–44	45–64	65+	DIFFERENCE BETWEEN 65+ AND 18–29	CORRELATION WITH AGE*
JAPAN	17	25	44	68	+51	.40
USA	17	29	45	63	+46	.36
NETHERLANDS	28	46	59	72	+44	.28
CANADA	13	27	46	55	+42	.30
FRANCE	37	50	66	78	+41	.30
SWEDEN	52	67	82	92	+40	.32
AUSTRIA	34	53	68	73	+39	.27
FINLAND	22	33	49	54	+32	.25
DENMARK	44	57	78	74	+30	.25
BELGIUM	27	40	58	57	+30	.21
GERMANY	42	60	68	70	+28	.18
UK	8	19	33	35	+23	.20
IRELAND	37	48	57	59	+22	.22
ITALY	37	48	57	59	+22	.13

*The "follow politics" variable has been recoded as follows for purposes of calculating correlations: every day = 7; several times a week = 3; once or twice a week = 1.5; less often = .5; never = 0.

Question wording: "How often do you follow politics in the news on TV, or on the radio, or in the daily newspapers?"

Source: 1999–2001 World Values Study.

they followed politics in the news every day compared to just 30 percent of young adults.

Because young people in other democracies are not following politics, they are not learning basic political facts either. An impressive collection of survey data collected between 1959 and 2002 in various countries shows how a generation gap in political knowledge has developed. We will examine data from four cross-national surveys: the Civic Culture Study (1959–1960), the Participation and Political Equality Study (1967–1971), the European Communities Study (1970), and the Comparative Study of Electoral Systems (1996–2002).

Being generally concerned with citizens' political competence, the Civic Culture Study attempted to measure how much political information respondents possessed. As Almond and Verba wrote, "Democratic competence is closely related to having valid information about political issues and processes, and to the ability to use information in the analysis of issues and the devising of influence strategies."[48] In their 1959–1960 surveys they employed two sets of open-ended questions in an effort to gauge how much respondents knew about the politics of their country. The first set asked respondents to name up to three party leaders from each of the major political parties in that country. The second set noted that new presidents or prime ministers were responsible for appointing people to cabinet positions and then asked respondents whether they could recall what some of these offices are. Table 3.8 displays the mean number of party leaders and cabinet offices that people within each age category successfully named. Looking across the rows, one can see that in every case, young respondents in these four countries displayed more political information than respondents over the age of 60. Controlling for education produces a positive correlation between political information and age in the United States, but not in West Germany and Italy, and for only one of the two measures in the United Kingdom.

TABLE 3.8

Political Knowledge by Age in Four Countries, Circa 1960

	18–30	31–40	41–60	61+	CORRELATION BETWEEN AGE AND KNOWLEDGE, CONTROLLING FOR EDUCATION
MEAN NUMBER OF PARTY LEADERS IDENTIFIED					
USA	3.8	4.2	4.0	3.7	.14
UK	2.9	3.2	3.1	2.4	.08
WEST GERMANY	4.6	4.7	4.5	4.4	−.01
ITALY	2.8	2.8	2.3	1.7	−.02
MEAN NUMBER OF CABINET OFFICES IDENTIFIED					
USA	2.9	3.1	2.8	2.3	.12
UK	3.3	3.4	3.1	2.0	−.08
WEST GERMANY	3.5	3.4	3.2	2.7	−.11
ITALY	2.0	2.0	1.4	1.1	−.02

Source: 1959–1960 Civic Culture Study.

Because the political information measures used in the Civic Culture Study were open-ended as opposed to specific factual questions, they may just reflect the ability to recall names. Fortunately, the follow-up study a decade later, called "Participation and Political Equality," asked a series of direct questions in Japan and the Netherlands, as well as the same open-ended questions about party leaders in Austria. In addition, the

1970 European Communities Study asked samples in five countries if they could name the members of the Common Market (EEC), as well as their country's prime minister and foreign minister.[49] Table 3.9 presents data by age from both of these studies.

TABLE 3.9
Political Knowledge by Age in Seven Countries, Circa 1970
[entries = percentage of acceptable answers]

	<30	30–44	45–64	65+	CORRELATION BETWEEN AGE AND KNOWLEDGE, CONTROLLING FOR EDUCATION
FRANCE 1970	58	59	63	57	.15
NETHERLANDS 1971	55	59	58	54	.10
BELGIUM 1970	55	55	58	43	.03
NETHERLANDS 1970	77	76	77	75	.02
AUSTRIA 1967	56	57	54	46	−.04
ITALY 1970	63	53	47	38	−.05
JAPAN 1967*	71	68	66	51	−.10
WEST GERMANY 1970	74	72	70	62	−.12

*Age categories for Japan were 20–29, 30–44, 45–59, 60+.

Netherlands 1971: Index based on questions asking respondents to identify the prime minister, and the ministers of foreign affairs, social affairs, development aid, and the treasury.

Japan 1967: Index based on asking respondents to identify the prime minister, the age one is eligible to vote in Diet elections, and the age one is eligible to run for the Diet.

Austria 1967: Index based on adding up the number of national OVP and SPO leaders that people could name, with the maximum of 8 equaling 100 percent correct.

All 1970 studies: A perfect score indicates naming all seven countries that were European Economic Community members at the time, as well as the prime minister and foreign minister of one's own country.

Sources: Participation and Political Equality Study, 1967–1971; European Communities Study, 1970.

The entries represent the percentage of acceptable answers. As was the case with the Civic Culture data, in every instance the elderly had the lowest score and in a few instances young adults scored the highest. The average correlation between political information and age, controlling for education, was .00—indicating that once education was held constant, there was no relationship at all between age and political knowledge as of about 1970.

In recent times, the picture has been quite different throughout the world's established democracies. Table 3.10 presents data from 12 established democracies for which political information items have recently been asked as part of the Comparative Study of Electoral Systems. The pattern of young adults being the least politically knowledgeable can now be readily seen in most of these countries. On average, young adults got the correct answer 43 percent of the time in the various national surveys presented in Table 3.10 compared to 55 percent for senior citizens. Controlling for education, the typical correlation between age and political knowledge was .21—almost as high as found recently in the United States.

Summary numbers of patterns of political knowledge are useful, but in order to really grasp the problem they represent, some specific examples will help to illustrate the phenomenon. Among the most interesting and telling differences I found were as follows:

- Seventy-three percent of Australian senior citizens knew that no one may stand for parliament unless they pay a deposit, compared to 27 percent of young adults.
- Eighty-one percent of Swiss senior citizens could name the president of the confederation, compared to 54 percent of young adults.

TABLE 3.10

Political Knowledge by Age in Established Democracies in Recent Years
[entries = average percentage of correct answers]

	18–29	30–44	45–64	65+	CORRELATION BETWEEN AGE AND KNOWLEDGE, CONTROLLING FOR EDUCATION
NEW ZEALAND 1996	41	46	61	67	.37
SWEDEN 1998	35	40	51	56	.33
NETHERLANDS 1998	41	48	57	56	.28
AUSTRALIA 1996	36	41	50	54	.27
UK 1997	51	63	69	68	.23
NORWAY 1997	38	45	53	54	.23
CANADA 1997	50	57	63	64	.23
IRELAND 2002	62	69	74	75	.23
FRANCE 2002	42	48	53	54	.21
SWEDEN 2002	37	47	54	52	.19
NEW ZEALAND 2002	42	47	53	55	.16
BELGIUM 1999	43	48	47	40	.11
GERMANY 1998	39	40	43	45	.10
SWITZERLAND 1999	46	49	54	53	.08
GERMANY 2002	36	35	39	37	.06

Source: Comparative Study of Electoral Systems.

- Eighty-three percent of German senior citizens could name the foreign minister, compared to 55 percent of young adults.
- Sixty-five percent of Canadian senior citizens could name the minister of finance, compared to 22 percent of young adults.

- Sixty percent of Swedish senior citizens could identify the photo of the leader of the Green Party, compared to 22 percent of young adults—even though young people were more likely to vote for this party.
- Eighty percent of Norwegian senior citizens could recall who had been president of the Storting (Parliament) for the last four years, compared to 39 percent of young adults.
- Sixty percent of Irish senior citizens could identify the name of Ireland's European commissioner, compared to 35 percent of young adults.
- Sixty percent of New Zealand senior citizens understood how the country's new mixed-member proportional (MMP) electoral system worked, compared to 34 percent of young adults.

Exceptions to the general pattern of the young being the least knowledgeable were rare, but there were some. In Canada, young people were 9 percent more likely to know who had been the country's first female prime minister; in Switzerland, the young were 10 percent more likely to know how many signatures are required for a referendum; in Germany, young people were 8 percent more likely to know the number of EU members; and in France, the young were 3 percent more likely to know that deputies were not elected via proportional representation. These political facts that young people were relatively aware of show that today's youth are not doomed to always be politically clueless. The problem is that these days, young people get such little exposure to political events and news reports that few such facts get through to them.

CONCLUSION: THE IMPACT OF POLITICAL KNOWLEDGE

It is hardly young people's fault that their generation has learned less about politics than any other generation since the beginning of survey research. It is often said in the culinary business, "You are what you eat." In the news business, it could well be said, "You know what you follow." And in the case of young adults, what they follow closely is entertainment, not politics. Therefore, surveys have found that young Americans are the most likely to know things like the winner of *American Idol*, the name of Homer Simpson's hometown, or who won the most recent Super Bowl.[50]

Regardless of whether the phenomenon of young people not following political news stems from deliberate or circumstantial avoidance, the relative lack of political knowledge that is the result has real consequences. Thomas Jefferson once said that there has never been, nor ever will be, a people who are politically ignorant and free. If this is indeed the case, write Stephen Bennett and Eric Rademacher, then "we can legitimately wonder what the future holds if Xers remain as uninformed as they are about government and public affairs."[51] While this may well be an overreaction, there definitely are important consequences when citizens lack political information. In *What Americans Know About Politics and Why It Matters*, Michael Delli Carpini and Scott Keeter make a strong case for the importance of staying informed about public affairs. Political knowledge, they argue: 1) fosters civic virtues, such as political tolerance; 2) helps citizens to identify what policies would truly benefit them and to incorporate this information in to their voting behavior; and 3) promotes active participation in politics.[52] It is certainly the case that due to youths' lacking information about politics compared to their elders, a significant generation gap has emerged in terms of turnout in many established democracies. This development will be examined in detail in the next chapter.

Appendix to Chapter 3

List of questions used for knowledge scales in Table 3.5.

1948: Respondents were asked the following set of questions: "Now, we'd like to find out a little bit of what people have heard about what is going on between ourselves and Russia. Do you happen to know whether the U.S. has been doing anything to try to stop Russia from getting control of other countries? What have we been doing? Have you heard anything about the troubles we have been having with Russia in Berlin? Do you happen to know whether we have been doing anything to help Western Germany get back on her feet? What are we doing?" Responses were coded in 1948 into the following four categories: no information, low information, medium information, and high information. In order to create a 0-to-100 scale, these categories have been recoded to 0, 33, 66, and 100.

1960: 1) where Nixon was from; 2) Nixon's age [40s]; 3) Nixon's class [middle]; 4) Nixon's religion [Protestant, Quaker]; 5) where JFK was from; 6) JFK's age [40s]; 7) JFK's class [upper]; 8) party in control of the House before the election; 9) party in control of the House after the election

1964: 1) where Goldwater was from; 2) where Johnson was from; 3) Goldwater's religion; 4) Johnson's religion; 5) party in control of the House before the election; 6) party in control of the House after the election; 7) whether Johnson had supported civil rights act; 8) whether Goldwater had supported civil rights act

1966: 1) able to name a Supreme Court justice; 2) party in control of the House before the election; 3) party in control of the House after the election

1968, 1976, 1980: 1) party in control of the House before the election; 2) party in control of the House after the election

1972: 1) know how many times a president can be elected; 2) know the length of a Senate term; 3) know the length of a House term; 4) party in control of the House before the election; 5) party in control of the House after the election

1984: 1) party in control of the House before the election; 2) party in control of the House after the election; 3) party in control of the Senate before the election; 4) party in control of the Senate after the election

1986: 1) identify Bush; 2) identify Weinberger; 3) identify Rehnquist; 4) identify Volcker; 5) identify Dole; 6) identify O'Neill; 7) party in control of the House before the election; 6) party in control of the Senate before the election

1988: 1) identify Ted Kennedy; 2) identify Schultz; 3) identify Rehnquist; 4) identify Gorbachev; 5) identify Thatcher; 6) identify Arafat; 7) identify Wright; 8) party in control of the House before the election; 9) party in control of the House after the election

1990: 1) identify Quayle; 2) identify George Mitchell; 3) identify Rehnquist; 4) identify Gorbachev; 5) identify Thatcher; 6) identify Mandela; 7) identify Foley; 8) party in control of the House before the election; 9) party in control of the House after the election

1992: 1) identify Quayle; 2) identify Rehnquist; 3) identify Yeltsin; 4) identify Foley; 5) know that the Supreme Court decides constitutionality; 6) know that the president nominates judges; 7) party in control of the House before the election; 8) party in control of the Senate before the election

1994: 1) identify Gore; 2) identify Rehnquist; 3) identify Yeltsin; 4) identify Foley; 5) know that the Supreme Court decides constitutionality; 6) know that the president nominates federal judges; 7) party in control of the House before the election; 8) party in control of the Senate before the election

1996: 1) identify Gore; 2) identify Rehnquist; 3) identify Yeltsin; 4) identify
      Gingrich; 5) party in control of House before the election; 6) party
      in control of House after the election

1998: 1) identify Gore; 2) identify Rehnquist; 3) identify Yeltsin; 4) identify
      Gingrich; 5) party in control of the House before the election; 6) party
      in control of the Senate before the election

2000: 1) where Bush was from; 2) where Gore was from; 3) party in control of
      the House before the election; 4) party in control of the Senate before the
      election; 5) Lieberman's religion [Jewish]; 6) identify William Rehnquist;
      7) identify Tony Blair; 8) identify Janet Reno; 9) identify Trent Lott

2004: 1) identify Hastert; 2) identify Cheney; 3) identify Blair; 4) identify
      Rehnquist; 5) House majority before the election; 6) Senate majority
      before the election

CHAPTER 4

Where Have All the
Young Voters Gone?

Why does anyone ever vote? Rational choice theorists have long pointed out that the chance of any one individual's vote making a difference to the outcome is extraordinarily slight. What instead drives many people to vote is simply that for one reason or another, they care who wins.[53] Such participation can be likened to spectators at a sporting event. Just like with voting, the involvement of any particular fan is hardly crucial to the outcome. While democracy wouldn't exist without some citizens going to the polls, without fans at a game there wouldn't be a home field advantage. Individually, a sports spectator gets the benefits of rooting in person for his or her team, enjoying the spectacle, and seeing firsthand who wins. Similar benefits can be posited for voters. People who have a clear personal interest in who governs and what the government does are therefore more inclined to vote, just as people with a favorite team are more likely to attend a sporting event involving their team.

But if you don't follow the sport and don't have a favorite team, then you are less likely to go to the games. Likewise in the world of politics, people who don't follow the news and current events are less likely to participate in elections for a number of similarly fundamental reasons. If you don't follow political news, then you are less likely to: 1) know who is running for various public offices; 2) be informed about what the candidates stand for; 3) have an interest in the issues that are being debated; and 4) realize what is at stake in an election—both for yourself personally as well as for the country. Thus with recent generations establishing modern lows for newspaper reading, TV news watching, and knowledge of public affairs (as shown in the previous three chapters), it is to be expected that their turnout rates should be falling substantially behind their elders.

Indeed, as this chapter shows, getting young adults to the polls these days is a lot like getting someone who generally doesn't follow sports to watch a football game. This problem is particularly evident in elections of lesser importance such as midterm elections, primaries, and local elections. These elections—commonly referred to in political science as "second-order elections"—attract less media attention. Therefore, people who pay minimal attention to politics often have little reason to care about them. Elections for the presidency of the United States or a nation's parliament, on the other hand, are more like the Super Bowl. Just as some people who don't follow football will end up watching the Super Bowl because of all the hoopla surrounding it, so will some people who rarely follow public affairs get caught up enough in election fever to vote. As will be seen in the first part of this chapter, getting young adults to vote in Super Bowl-style elections (commonly referred to as "first-order elections" in political science) is becoming more and more of a problem in the United States and many other established democracies. The second part of this chapter then turns to second-order elections, where the age gap in terms of electoral participation has reached alarming levels in many countries.

TURNOUT BY AGE IN AMERICAN PRESIDENTIAL ELECTIONS SINCE 1964

In 1964, the U.S. Census Bureau began a series of studies regarding registration and turnout in U.S. elections. A primary motivation of the Census Bureau in examining this topic was to measure racial differences in turnout that were widely perceived to be a blemish on the practice of American democracy. Blacks at the time were substantially underrepresented at the polls, and the 1964 Census Bureau study provided some hard data on the state of the problem. In the South, this survey found that 59 percent of Whites reported that they had voted, compared to just 44 percent among non-Whites. In the standard shorthand used throughout this chapter, such a turnout discrepancy translates into a turnout ratio of about 1.3 to 1. Or, to put it another way, southern Whites were roughly 30 percent more likely to vote than were southern non-Whites in 1964. Such a large gap in turnout rates no doubt helped persuade the U.S. Congress to end racial discrimination in registration practices in the South by passing the 1965 Voting Rights Act.

Interestingly, the cover page of the Census Bureau's report regarding turnout in 1964 highlighted turnout differences between the young and the old, perhaps because this was a much less expected finding.[54] A careful reading of this report reveals that the difference between the national turnout rate of 21- to 24-year-olds and those over 65 in 1964 was just as wide as the racial differences in the South. This finding validated the concerns about low youth turnout expressed by President Kennedy's Commission on Registration and Voting Participation. The Commission's November 1963 report argued that by the time young people turn 21, many "are so far removed from the stimulation of the educational process that their interest in public affairs has waned." The report went on to warn that "Some may be lost as voters for the rest of their lives," and to recommend that in order to address this problem, "states should carefully consider reducing the minimum voting age to 18."[55]

As the movement to lower the voting age to 18 grew in strength over the next eight years, the general sense of opinion was that this would ameliorate the problem of relatively low youth turnout—not make it worse. Jane Eisner's summary of the Senate Judiciary Committee hearings on the proposal concludes that there was "a palpable belief that these new voters would improve the political system with their intelligence, idealism, and energy."[56] Historian Alexander Keyssar notes that the ratification process for the Twenty-sixth Amendment, which lowered the voting age to 18, was the fastest in American history.[57] When this amendment was certified in 1971, President Nixon remarked, "The country needs an infusion of new spirit from time to time. As I stand here, I sense that we can have confidence that America's new voters will provide what this country needs."[58]

Such high hopes for voting participation among 18- to 20-year-olds were quickly dispelled when this group was first able to vote in the Nixon-McGovern contest of 1972, as their turnout rate of 48 percent was the lowest for any age group that year. Ironically, what was then a disappointing result for the 18- to 20-year-old turnout now looks impressive in light of subsequent results. As can be seen from the Census Bureau's survey data displayed in Table 4.1, in the eight elections since 1972, the turnout rate of 18- to 20-year-olds has averaged just 35 percent. Given that the turnout rate for the under-21 crowd has consistently been the lowest of any age group, the lowering of the voting age has clearly contributed to the downturn in U.S. turnout in recent decades.

TABLE 4.1
Turnout by Age in Presidential Elections, 1964–2004

	18–20	21–24	25–34	35–44	45–54	55–64	65+	65+ / 21–24 RATIO
1964	—	51	65	73	76	76	66	1.3 : 1
1968	—	50	63	71	75	75	66	1.3 : 1
1972	48	51	60	66	71	71	64	1.3 : 1
1976	38	46	55	63	68	70	62	1.3 : 1
1980	36	43	55	64	68	71	65	1.5 : 1
1984	37	44	55	64	68	72	68	1.5 : 1
1988	33	38	48	61	67	69	69	1.8 : 1
1992	39	46	53	64	69	72	70	1.5 : 1
1996	31	33	43	55	62	68	67	2.0 : 1
2000	28	35	44	55	62	67	68	1.9 : 1
2004	41	42	47	57	64	70	69	1.7 : 1

Source: U.S. Census Bureau surveys.

It might be theorized that 18- to 20-year-olds will always vote in substantially lesser numbers than people a few years older due to life cycle factors. Highton and Wolfinger outline a series of major life changes that people under the age of 25 commonly go through while they sort out their lives, each of which might make it less likely for them to vote.[59] However, their analysis of the 1996 Census turnout data set demonstrates that such lifestyle transitions can account for only a small portion of the age differential in turnout. Thus, it would be a mistake to conclude that low turnout among 18- to 20-year-olds was inevitable, and should have been foreseen by the advocates of the Twenty-sixth Amendment. Indeed, there have been three cases—1972, 1996, and 2004—in which the turnout rate for Americans under the age of 21 was not significantly different from the rate for those between the ages of 21 and 24.

The problem with getting America's youngest eligible voters to the polls has been that they have gotten the least exposure to political events while growing up due to the ongoing changes in media habits outlined in previous chapters. As these changes in the media environment have played out over the years, the age distribution of Americans who participate in presidential elections has become much more skewed toward the elderly. Between 1964 and 1976, the ratio between the turnout rate of people over 65 and that of those between the ages of 21 and 24 was a consistent 1.3 to 1. Since then, this ratio has gotten much worse, reaching a high of 2.0 to 1 in the particularly dull 1996 contest between Clinton and Dole. The 2004 election saw a modest improvement to a 1.7 to 1 ratio, as turnout rose most notably among the young (who, of course, had the most potential for such an increase due to their previous abysmal turnout rates). But in spite of this recent upsurge of electoral participation among young adults, the situation remains a sorry one for American democracy. If a 1.3 to 1 turnout ratio between Whites and Blacks in the South was a dreadful state of affairs in the early 1960s, then a 1.7 to 1 ratio between the old and the young is certainly a serious problem in the early twenty-first century.

Furthermore, the problem of lower turnout is no longer mostly confined to the under-25 age group. Even with the increase in turnout rates in 2004, the majority of people between the ages of 25 and 34 still did not vote. Whereas differences in turnout between this age group and seniors were negligible in 1964 and 1968, seniors were more than 1.6 times as likely to vote as those aged 25 to 34 in 2004. A similar transformation can be found among Americans between the ages of 35 to 44. Between 1964 and 1976, this group consistently had a higher turnout rate than people over 65. Since then, a substantial gap has opened up, as turnout among this middle-aged group has fallen dramatically. In each of the last three presidential elections, the ratio between the turnout rate of seniors and the 35-to-44-year-old group has been 1.2 to 1.

In short, there has been a dramatic change in the relationship between age and turnout since the Census Bureau surveys started keeping track of who votes in America. Because these surveys have a huge sample size of roughly 100,000 cases, it is possible to graph participation rates by age quite precisely. Figure 4.1 presents smoothed curves for the age-turnout relationship in three elections: 1972, 1996, and 2004. In 1972 (the first year for which precise age data are available given that the raw data for the 1964 and 1968 surveys have been lost), one can see that

FIGURE 4.1

U.S. Turnout by Age: 1972, 1996, and 2004

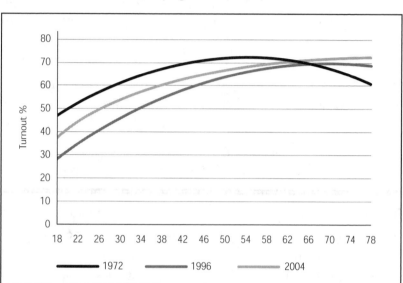

Source: U.S. Census Bureau surveys.

turnout went up gradually about 20 percentage points from age 18 to age 44, then leveled off, and finally started to decline after the age of 60. In 1996, the lowest turnout election in recent times, turnout went up far more steeply with age, rising about 40 percentage points from age 18 to age 60 and then leveling off at a rate of about 70 percent through age 80. Finally, the age-turnout curve for 2004 illustrates how an increase in turnout is now bound to come mostly from the youngest adults. Yet, even the extraordinary intensity with which the 2004 presidential election was contested failed to motivate young and middle-aged

Americans to go to the polls in nearly the same percentages as seen in the landslide 1972 contest. In contrast, turnout rates among senior citizens were actually higher in both recent years shown in Figure 4.1 than in 1972. Political scientists used to write that the frailties of old age led to a decline in turnout after one became eligible for Social Security. Now an examination of the Census survey data shows that such a decline occurs only after 80 years of age. (Due to the way the Census Bureau codes these age categories together, these data are not displayed in the figure).[60] The greater access to medical care provided to today's seniors must surely be given some of the credit for this change, helping to keep them in sufficiently good health to vote. One could certainly tell young citizens this today as an illustration of how politics really can make a difference.

The changing relationship between age and turnout that has been found in the United States leads us to question whether a life cycle actually exists for electoral participation. A true life cycle pattern would be roughly the same throughout different time periods. This is not to imply that turnout should remain exactly the same over time, but rather that the participation of each age group should change by roughly the same amount from year to year. Clearly, this has not been the case in the United States.

Comparative data provide a key test for the existence of a life cycle effect for turnout. If one's stage in life really influences one's likelihood of voting, then this pattern should be found to be similar over time in most established democracies. We thus now turn to an examination of participation patterns in first-order elections in other countries.

TURNOUT BY AGE IN PARLIAMENTARY ELECTIONS: CHANGE OVER THREE DECADES

The early comparative research on parliamentary elections hardly mentioned turnout at all. Scholarly neglect of this subject occurred mainly because unlike in the United States, turnout levels were typically very high elsewhere in the established democratic world. With almost everyone voting, there was not much concern about analyzing the relatively small percentage of people who didn't vote. If American reformers who advocated lowering the voting age had found it difficult to conceive how expanding the franchise might lessen overall turnout levels, then those who advocated a similar move around the same time in other countries would have found it downright implausible. Turnout problems were something that America might have due to its burdensome registration procedures, but other established democracies (except tiny Switzerland) had no such worries. Citizens who were eligible to vote almost always did so; it mattered little whether they were young or old.

Table 4.2 presents turnout data by age group from surveys conducted circa 1972 in 16 established democracies. This time frame was selected for two reasons: 1) it was about the time when many other countries also lowered their voting age to 18; and 2) it was the earliest time period for which survey data on elections were available from almost all of the world's established democracies.[61] Looking down the column for people under 30, one can clearly see that most countries had no trouble at all in getting young people to the polls in this era. Only the United States and Switzerland had turnout rates below 80 percent among young adults. Excluding

TABLE 4.2

Percent Reporting Casting a Ballot by Age in Established Democracies, Circa 1972

	<30	30–44	45–64	65+	OLDEST/ YOUNGEST RATIO
USA 1972	53	65	71	64	1.2 : 1
SWITZERLAND 1971	48	66	67	55	1.1 : 1
GREAT BRITAIN FEB. 1974	82	88	92	89	1.1 : 1
FINLAND 1972	85	91	95	90	1.1 : 1
NETHERLANDS 1972	85	90	92	90	1.1 : 1
NORWAY 1969	90	94	97	94	1.0 : 1
CANADA 1974	83	83	88	86	1.0 : 1
ITALY 1972	95	97	96	97	1.0 : 1
AUSTRIA 1971	97	97	98	99	1.0 : 1
NEW ZEALAND 1975	93	97	98	95	1.0 : 1
DENMARK 1971	91	96	94	91	1.0 : 1
FRANCE 1967	89	90	92	89	1.0 : 1
SWEDEN 1973	92	95	95	92	1.0 : 1
JAPAN 1967	81	93	93	80	1.0 : 1
IRELAND 1977	82	88	83	79	1.0 : 1
GERMANY 1972	98	98	97	95	1.0 : 1

Notes: The voting age in Finland, Sweden, and Japan was 20; in Norway, France, Denmark, Italy, and Switzerland it was 21; all others had voting age of 18. Data from Ireland represent the percentage saying they were "certain to vote." The Irish age categories were 18–34, 35–44, 45–64, 65+. Age categories for Denmark were 21–29, 30–49, 50–64, 65+.

Sources: Various National Election Studies; U.S. Census Bureau Study; Finland, Austria, and Italy: Political Action Study; Ireland: NOP Preelection Poll.

these two outliers, the average reported turnout rate for people under 30 was a very healthy 89 percent during the period around 1972. Granted, this represents an overreport of voting turnout, as surveys commonly find that more people say they voted than we know actually did. However, there is no reason to suspect that young people would have been consistently more likely to over-report turnout than older people. And the key finding in the circa 1972 data is that there was not much of a discrepancy between the turnout rates of the elderly and the young. The United States was the only country in which the ratio between the two groups was above 1.1 to 1; in 11 of the 16 countries, the two groups had roughly equal turnout levels. To those who take a defeatist attitude regarding the current problem of low youth turnout and argue that this is just a difficult time in life to get people to go to the polls, these data send a clear message: not so long ago the participation rate of young people in parliamentary elections was quite healthy.

Today, the picture is markedly different in many countries. The United States is certainly not alone in having a problem getting young people to the polls. Table 4.3 presents recent data from 18 established democracies. In nine of these countries, people over 65 were at least 1.3 times more likely to have voted than adults under the age of 30. Or, if one simply looks at percentages, one finds that the turnout rate of young adults was at least 10 percent below that of senior citizens in 11 countries. Of the other seven established democracies covered in Table 4.3, Belgium and Australia require all citizens to show up at the polls for national elections. Only Italy, Austria, Sweden, Denmark, and the Netherlands have recently been successful in getting young people to vote in satisfactory numbers without compelling them to do so. Why these countries have not experienced the problem of low youth turnout is an interesting puzzle that I leave to others to investigate.[62] For the purposes of this book, the major point I want to get across is that the problem of low youth turnout is by no

TABLE 4.3

Percent Reporting Casting a Ballot by Age Categories in Advanced Industrialized Democracies in Recent Years

	<30	30–44	45–64	65+	OLDEST/YOUNGEST RATIO
JAPAN 2003*	36	55	71	71	2.0 : 1
USA 2000	36	52	64	68	1.9 : 1
GREAT BRITAIN 2001*	39	57	69	71	1.8 : 1
IRELAND 2002	59	82	87	87	1.5 : 1
CANADA 2000	63	82	91	92	1.5 : 1
NORWAY 2001*	59	78	82	84	1.4 : 1
NEW ZEALAND 2002*	63	76	84	88	1.4 : 1
SWITZERLAND 2003	57	57	72	81	1.4 : 1
FRANCE 2002	67	78	86	84	1.3 : 1
FINLAND 2003	68	80	87	83	1.2 : 1
GERMANY 2002*	70	79	83	82	1.2 : 1
AUSTRIA 2002	82	90	92	90	1.1 : 1
SWEDEN 1998	83	89	91	90	1.1 : 1
NETHERLANDS 1998	88	91	92	94	1.1 : 1
DENMARK 2001*	81	85	89	83	1.0 : 1
AUSTRALIA 2004**	97	98	98	99	1.0 : 1
ITALY 2001	89	92	93	86	1.0 : 1
BELGIUM 2004**	89	98	97	92	1.0 : 1

*Validated records of actual participation used here
**Compulsory voting in effect

Notes: Age categories were slightly different for the following countries—Germany: 18-29, 30-44, 45-60, 60+; Ireland: 18-34, 35-44, 45-64, 65+; Norway, Denmark: 18-29, 30-39, 40-59, 60+.

Sources: Comparative Study of Electoral Systems unless otherwise noted; Italy, Austria, and Finland: European Social Survey 2002/3; New Zealand Election Study; British Election Study; U.S. Census Bureau Study; Irish Central Statistics Office; Statistiches Bundesamt (Germany); Statistics Norway; Japan National Election Management Commission; Jorgen Elklit, Palle Svensson, and Lise Togeby, "Why Is Voter Turnout Not Declining in Denmark?" Paper presented at the 2005 APSA meeting.

means just an American one. To those who propose explanations for why turnout rates have gone down among young Americans based on particular events in U.S. politics, I ask them to consider why similar trends can also be found in Japan, Great Britain, Ireland, Canada, Norway, New Zealand, Switzerland, France, Finland, and Germany.

THE TURNOUT GAP IN AMERICAN SECOND-ORDER ELECTIONS

As Mark Franklin writes, "Turnout appears to vary because of variations in the character of elections."[63] Franklin insightfully points out that what differentiates low from high turnout elections are not the characteristics of the eligible electorate but rather the nature of the elections themselves. Because second-order elections are less likely to decide crucial issues, or get as much media coverage as presidential or parliamentary elections, they just don't appear as important to citizens. And when elections don't appear important, individuals who are less attuned to political news may not hear enough about them to feel that they have any stake in who wins. As outlined in the first three chapters, young adults these days are particularly likely to fit this description. Hence, it should be expected that age differences in turnout will be even larger in second-order elections than in first-order ones.

Five U.S. states now regularly report voting participation rates of registered voters within various age categories. Advances in computer technology have made it relatively simple to computerize voter registration lists. Given that citizens are required to state their date of birth in order to establish their eligibility to vote, age is one variable that is always included in these computerized records. Once an election is completed, local registrars add information regarding who voted, which is a crucial piece of information for them because Congress has specified that no one can be purged from a registration list if he or she has voted in the past four years.[64] With these columns of data in their computer banks, a basic cross-tabulation reveals precisely how many of those registered within each age group actually voted. Table 4.4 presents the data on turnout by age that Iowa, Georgia, Delaware, South Carolina, and Alaska have reported on their Web sites for elections held between 2000 and 2004. It should be noted that these percentages are based only on people who have gone to the trouble of getting on the voter registration rolls. Were one to take into account the fact that young Americans are the least likely to be registered, the turnout gap between the young and the old would be even greater than that displayed in Table 4.4. However, the major point of this table is to illustrate differences between types of elections, and these official turnout statistics clearly show that young people's participation rates fall off the most sharply when elections are not hotly contested.

Age bias at the polls was far more pronounced in the 2002 midterm election than in either of the presidential elections in all five states. The data from Iowa provide a perfect example. As can be seen in the upper-right corner of Table 4.4, the ratio between the turnout rate of senior citizens and those aged 18 to 24 in Iowa increased from 1.9 : 1 in the 2000 election to 3.3 : 1 in the 2002 midterm election. Although the turnout of seniors in Iowa had the most room for drop-off, given their high turnout in 2000, their participation remained strong in 2002—falling slightly from 83 to

TABLE 4.4

Official Turnout Figures of Registered Voters by Age in Presidential Versus Second-Order Elections in Five States, 2000–2004

	18–24	25–34	35–49	50–64	65+	OLDEST/YOUNGEST RATIO
IA 2004	58	61	78	86	84	1.4 : 1
IA 2000	44	54	75	84	83	1.9 : 1
IA 2002	22	35	58	72	73	3.3 : 1

	18–24	25–29	30–34	35–39	40–44	45–49	50–54	55–59	60–64	65+	OLDEST/YOUNGEST RATIO
GA 2004	56	63	71	75	77	79	81	83	84	80	1.4 : 1
GA 2000	44	55	64	69	72	75	78	79	81	77	1.8 : 1
GA 2002	22	33	44	51	56	60	65	68	71	68	3.1 : 1

	18–29	30–39	40–49	50–64	65+	OLDEST/YOUNGEST RATIO
DE 2004	55	57	68	77	75	1.4 : 1
DE 2000	48	58	70	80	76	1.6 : 1
DE 2002	19	31	46	59	64	3.4 : 1

	18–21	22–44	45–64	65+	OLDEST/YOUNGEST RATIO
SC 2004	62	63	77	74	1.2 : 1
SC 2000	49	55	73	70	1.4 : 1
SC 2002	28	43	65	67	2.4 : 1
SC 2004 PRIMARY	13	15	31	39	3.0 : 1
SC 2000 PRIMARY	9	11	24	31	3.4 : 1
SC 2002 PRIMARY	10	16	30	39	3.9 : 1

	18–24	25–34	34–44	45–54	55–64	65+	OLDEST/YOUNGEST RATIO
AK 2004	53	55	66	74	76	75	1.4 : 1
AK 2000	46	48	61	69	70	70	1.5 : 1
AK 2002	26	35	51	63	67	66	2.5 : 1
AK 2004 PRIMARY	11	14	24	35	43	48	4.4 : 1
AK 2002 PRIMARY	9	12	21	31	36	40	4.4 : 1
AK 2000 PRIMARY	7	8	15	22	28	35	5.0 : 1

Sources: Secretary of State Web sites for Iowa, Georgia, Delaware, South Carolina, and Alaska.

73 percent. In contrast, turnout among young Iowans who were registered was cut in half, dropping from a rather poor showing of 44 percent in 2000 to an abysmal 22 percent in 2002. The dreadful turnout of young Iowans in 2002 was unfortunately quite typical of the pattern throughout the country. Looking at the other four states shown in Table 4.4 reveals that the highest turnout rate among the youngest age category was 28 percent for 18- to 21-year-olds in South Carolina.

Yet, the poor midterm participation rate among young Americans looks relatively rosy compared to their widespread neglect of primary elections. The states of South Carolina and Alaska consistently reported turnout rates of about 10 percent for the youngest age group in 2000, 2002, and 2004. By contrast, the typical turnout rate for senior citizens in primaries in these states was about 40 percent. One reason that young Americans often do not participate in primaries is that in many states they are closed to voters who are not registered as Democrats or Republicans, and young people are the most likely to be political independents. But each of these two states allows independents to choose a ballot from one or the other party for primary elections even though they aren't registered as a member of that party. Nevertheless, young registered citizens seem to treat primary elections like a party they have not been invited to. The result is that older voters are largely in charge of picking the candidates who will appear on the November ballot.

Although most of the data in Table 4.4 regarding young Americans' voting participation rates reflect bad news, there is one recent bright spot in the official turnout statistics from these five states. The figures from the 2004 general election demonstrate that when a close and interesting contest for president occurs, the turnout of young people will go up dramatically (at least among those who are registered). The problem is that this is the exception, not the rule. In the complex, multilayered American political system, which provides for frequent opportunities to go to the polls, most elections are second-order ones. Just tuning in to a particularly exciting Super Bowl doesn't make one a football fan; similarly, just participating in one especially hotly contested election doesn't make a group an integral part of the American political process. As the National Football League and its sponsors make plans for its next season, they are hardly likely to take into account the views of people who tuned in only to the Super Bowl. Likewise, politicians are bound to pay only marginal attention to voters who show up only for a high-intensity presidential election, concentrating far more on people who can be counted on to vote on a regular basis.

The widespread availability of voting history records enables political campaign strategists to quite easily identify these habitual voters. Traditional party organizations who used to sweep whole neighborhoods have been largely replaced by more sophisticated voter targeting. As Alan Ware has written, this switch from party to high-tech campaigning "helped to create 'two nations' in the electorate: those who received considerable attention from candidates and those who were ignored."[65] Many campaigns will bother to contact only those voters who have regularly shown up at the polls in past elections. Such a focus creates a mobilization bias in favor of older voters.

An analysis of 5,354,376 actual voter history records between 2000 and 2003 from Los Angeles, San Francisco, and Orange County, California, illustrates just how pronounced this bias is.[66]

Table 4.5 displays the percentage of registered voters in each age category who voted in all three major contests from 2000 to 2003—the 2000 presidential election, the 2002 midterm election, and the 2003 recall election that made Arnold Schwarzenegger governor. Among those who were 18 to 24 years old (as of 2000) and registered to vote in California throughout this whole period, only 14 percent voted in all three elections. By contrast, among citizens who were between 65 and 79 years of age, an impressive 60 percent voted three out of three times. The electoral participation age gap appears even wider once one takes into account the proportion of each age that was registered to vote. As California campaigns geared up for the 2004 primary, the odds of a citizen

TABLE 4.5
Percent Voting in All Three Major Elections From 2000 to 2003 in Los Angeles, San Francisco, and Orange County, California, by Age

	18–24	25–34	35–44	45–54	55–64	65–79	80+
PERCENT OF THOSE WHO WERE REGISTERED WHO ACTUALLY VOTED IN ALL THREE ELECTIONS	14	25	40	50	56	60	47
PERCENT OF CITIZENS REGISTERED ACCORDING TO CENSUS SURVEY	43	59	67	72	76	79	75
ESTIMATED PERCENT OF CITIZENS WHO VOTED IN ALL THREE ELECTIONS	6	15	27	36	43	47	35

Note: Age is as of the 2000 election.

Sources: Voter registration records of Los Angeles, San Francisco, and Orange County; 2002 Census Bureau Survey.

born between 1921 and 1935 being on a target list of regular voters would have been about one in two, compared to just one in eight for citizens born between 1966 and 1975, and a mere one in 20 for those born between 1976 and 1982.

The impact of being able to identify regular voters via these computerized lists is likely to be cumulative over time. Older citizens get their participatory habits reinforced because campaigns continually ask them for their votes, whereas many younger citizens never get into the habit of voting because campaigns consider contacting them to be a poor investment of resources. The result is a classic "catch-22" situation—many younger people won't vote until a campaign mobilizes them, but many campaigns won't focus on them because they haven't established a history of voting participation. Such an effect is most likely to be seen in second-order elections over time, as these are the types of elections for which many people need a bit of a push before they will participate.

There are two types of American second-order elections for which time series turnout data can be examined—midterm elections and presidential primary elections. Table 4.6 presents data from the Census Bureau studies of midterm elections from 1966 to 2002. The patterns are much the same as found for presidential elections (see Table 4.1), except they are more pronounced. Despite starting from a substantially lower level in the mid-1960s, electoral participation by the youngest groups has fallen off even more sharply in midterm elections. The turnout rates of both the 21-to-24- and 25-to-34-year-old categories have been almost cut in half between 1966 and 2002. With seniors voting at slightly greater levels than in past midterm elections, the generational gap has grown to stunning levels.

TABLE 4.6
Turnout by Age in Midterm Elections, 1966–2002

	18–20	21–24	25–34	35–44	45–54	55–64	65+	65+ / 21–24 RATIO
1966	—	32	46	60	64	65	56	1.8 : 1
1970	—	30	41	50	58	64	57	1.9 : 1
1974	21	26	37	49	56	58	55	2.1 : 1
1978	20	26	38	50	56	61	56	2.2 : 1
1982	20	28	40	52	60	64	60	2.1 : 1
1986	19	24	35	49	55	63	60	2.5 : 1
1990	18	22	34	48	53	59	60	2.7 : 1
1994	17	22	32	46	55	59	61	2.8 : 1
1998	14	20	28	41	51	58	60	3.0 : 1
2002	15	19	27	40	50	57	61	3.2 : 1

Source: U.S. Census Bureau surveys.

Many observers thought that Al Qaeda's attack on American soil and the ongoing war against terrorism would reinvigorate electoral participation in America, especially among the young. But just over a year after the events of September 11 and as America prepared for an invasion of Iraq, less than one out of five Americans under the age of 25 bothered to vote, compared to three out of five people over the age of 65. It has long been said that old men send young men off to die in wars. What this has commonly referred to in a democracy is that older politicians who have worked their way up to high-level political offices are usually the ones who make these life-and-death decisions. But in the case of the first post-9/11 American national election, there was a deeper meaning evident, as it was older Americans who dominated the process of choosing the nation's Congress in 2002.

Ironically, it was young people's dissatisfaction with their lack of say toward American policy regarding the Vietnam War that was the impetus for a recent major expansion of second-order election opportunities in the United States. Presidential primaries were adopted by many states after young antiwar Americans found their voices muffled in 1968 due to undemocratic procedures commonly used at that time to select national convention delegates. As can be seen in the data displayed in Table 4.7, the participation gap between young and old in presidential primaries during the 1970s was roughly the same as could be found in general elections. However, since then, age has become far more related to primary turnout, as young people's participation rate in primaries has stayed about the same, whereas older people have

TABLE 4.7
Turnout in Presidential Primaries/Caucuses by Age, 1972–2000

	18–29	30–44	45–64	65+	OLDEST/YOUNGEST RATIO
1972	17	23	28	28	1.6 : 1
1976	20	27	31	25	1.3 : 1
1980	15	26	38	38	2.5 : 1
1988	18	36	44	47	2.6 : 1
1992	13	31	41	41	3.2 : 1
2000	18	37	54	62	3.4 : 1

Sources: 1972–1992 American National Election Study; 2000 National Annenberg Election Study.

become substantially more likely to turn out to choose the presidential nominees. The 2000 National Annenberg Election Study found that 62 percent of senior citizens reported voting in their state's presidential primary, compared to just 18 percent among respondents less than 30 years of age.

If it is fair to generalize that young Americans mostly yawn when given the opportunity to participate in midterm congressional elections and presidential primaries, then one can say that most are fast asleep when it comes to local elections. Localities are the basic building blocs of American democracy, and decisions made by local government are arguably the most relevant to citizens' day-to-day lives in America's relatively decentralized political system. Yet, due to the dearth of media attention to local politics, the vast majority of Americans do not participate in elections that are limited to just their own communities. Young people, because they are more mobile and often have less in the way of roots in the community, are particularly unlikely to be aware of local issues, and hence are relatively uninvolved in local politics.

One especially telling example of this pattern can be found in some 2003 participation data posted on the Internet by the town clerk of Concord, Massachusetts. One of the historic sites of the American Revolution, Concord continues to follow the traditional New England style of local participatory democracy. Just like in the revolutionary period, Concord continues to hold regular town meetings where everyone can have a say about the issues facing the town and can vote on specific motions. In addition, there are also regular elections for positions in the town's government, and occasionally to decide referendum issues.

Concord's town clerk reported election participation by age group throughout 2003, as well as the actual number of citizens in each age category who were known to be living there (whether registered to vote or not). The results for two town meetings and three town elections held during 2003 are displayed in Table 4.8. From these data, it is clear that one answer to the question of "Who runs Concord?" is that older people do, with ratios of participation between the oldest and youngest groups regularly exceeding 8 to 1. Of course, this is not due to any conspiracy to deny younger adults the rights that eighteenth-century citizens of Concord fought for. Rather, it is simply due to twenty-first-century American youths' neglect of local government.

TABLE 4.8
Who Runs Concord? Turnout by Age in 2003

	18–29	30–39	40–49	50–59	60–69	70+	OLDEST/ YOUNGEST RATIO
TOWN ELECTION MAY 2003	6	23	40	36	51	43	7.2 : 1
TOWN ELECTION SEPTEMBER 2003	5	20	37	35	48	42	8.4 : 1
TOWN ELECTION MARCH 2003	4	12	22	25	36	34	8.5 : 1
TOWN MEETING AUGUST 2003	1	3	7	8	11	9	9.0 : 1
TOWN MEETING APRIL 2003	1	8	14	13	16	12	12.0 : 1

Source: Clerk of Concord, MA, official registration and turnout statistics.

THE TURNOUT GAP IN SECOND-ORDER ELECTIONS IN OTHER ESTABLISHED DEMOCRACIES

The pattern of seniors' substantially outvoting young adults in second-order elections is hardly unique to American politics. Table 4.9 presents turnout data by age for a variety of regional and local elections around the world for which I have been able to find either survey data or official reports of participation by age. In Great Britain, a key part of New Labour's program for governing since they came to power in 1997 has been their policy of devolution, that is, passing some powers from the national government to newly formed local political institutions. Because devolution created new electoral opportunities, it cannot be said that the elderly were more likely to vote just out of habit. Nevertheless, senior citizens were roughly twice as likely to vote in elections for the new Scottish and Welsh Parliaments, as well as for London's first-ever mayoral election, than adults under the age of 25. A similar pattern of participation by age can be found in British Columbia, where provincial elections have long been very important, given the fact that Canadian provinces have retained power over many policy arenas that are the purview of Britain's national government. On the other side of the Pacific, the 2001 election for the city council of Christchurch, New Zealand, had an even stronger age bias, with the oldest age category being 4.5 times more likely to vote than the youngest group. And even though Norway is about as far away as one can get geographically from the South Island of New Zealand (site of Christchurch), the participation of young people in the 2003 Norwegian municipal elections was similarly disappointing.

TABLE 4.9

Turnout in Various Regional and Local Elections Around the World by Age

	18–24	25–34	35–44	45–54	55–64	65+	OLDEST/ YOUNGEST RATIO
SCOTTISH ASSEMBLY, 2003	42	41	51	59	66	75	1.8 : 1
WELSH ASSEMBLY, 1999	36	39	52	67	70	72	2.0 : 1
LONDON MAYOR, 2000	27	37	51	57	58	62	2.3 : 1
BRITISH COLUMBIA PROVINCIAL, 2001	27	39	54	63	69	71	2.6 : 1
WESTERN AUSTRALIA LOCAL, 2003*	19	20	29	36	47	55	2.9 : 1
CHRISTCHURCH, NZ, CITY COUNCIL, 2001	20	30	45	62	75	89	4.5 : 1

	18–25	26–29	30–39	40–49	50–59	60+	
NORWEGIAN MUNICIPAL, 2003*	18	19	30	40	43	45	2.5 : 1

*Validated records of actual participation used here

Sources: Christchurch = http://www.ccc.govt.nz/Elections/VotingAndNonVotingIn ChristchurchCity_October2001.pdf; British Columbia = http://www.elections.bc.ca/eac/ 2001VPStats_Summary.pdf; 2000 MORI survey of London for UK Electoral Commission; 1999 Welsh National Assembly Election Study; 2003 Scottish National Assembly Election Study; Western Australian Electoral Commission; Statistics Norway = http://statbank.ssb.no/ statistikkbanken/Default_FR.asp?tilside=selecttable/hovedtabellHjem.asp&KortnavnWeb= kommvalg&PLanguage=1&nvl=true&direkte=1&PXSid=0.

The data from Western Australia's local elections in 2003 merit special attention. Unlike the case for federal elections in Australia, for which participation is compulsory, Western Australians are free to choose whether or not to vote in local elections.[67] It might be hypothesized that because young

Australians have had the experience of regularly going to the polls for national elections (which occur at least once every three years in Australia), they should be more likely to vote in local elections than young people elsewhere. The fact that Western Australia conducts its local elections entirely by mail should further facilitate the participation of young adults, making it possible for them to vote without having to take time off from work or school. Nevertheless, when the Western Australian Electoral Commission examined the records of who sent in their ballots in 2003, it found that less than 20 percent of people under the age of 35 did so, as compared to 55 percent of senior citizens.[68] Apparently, the act of voting in first-order elections does not necessarily establish a habit of voting which predisposes young adults to vote in second-order elections.

Finally, the question remains as to whether, like in the United States, generational differences in participation in second-order elections have widened in most established democracies. The best data for examining this question are from elections for the European Parliament. Although European parliamentary elections may seem to loom larger than national elections in that they involve voters from numerous countries all going to the polls at about the same time, they nevertheless have all the characteristics of a second-order election. Far less media attention is paid to these elections than national parliamentary elections, and the general feeling is that less is at stake. As a result, public information about European elections is shockingly low. For example, when a sample of European Union citizens was asked in 2002 whether "members of the European Parliament are elected by citizens like you and me," only 43 percent correctly answered that this was a true statement.[69] With such a lack of knowledge about these elections, it should not be surprising that fewer people vote in them compared to national parliamentary elections in the same countries, befitting their classification as second-order elections. And as the novelty of European parliamentary elections has worn off since they were first held in 1979, turnout in them has fallen off substantially.[70]

A comparison of turnout figures by age in the European parliamentary elections of 1979 and 1999 reveals that young Europeans have contributed disproportionately to turnout decline in these elections.[71] Table 4.10 presents turnout data from all the countries that participated in both elections except for Belgium, which practices compulsory voting and hence has no turnout problems. In six of the seven countries, the ratio of participation between the oldest and youngest groups increased between 1979 and 1999. Countries such as France, Great Britain, and the Netherlands, which had some age disparity in European election turnout in 1979, had greater disparities 20 years later. And countries that had roughly equal turnout rates by age in the first European parliamentary elections, such as West Germany, Denmark, and Ireland, had substantial differences by 1999. Only Italy did not have a problem in getting adults under the age of 30 to the polls for the 1999 European parliamentary elections. The case of Italy can best be interpreted as demonstrating once again that when turnout is very high in a society, young adults are swept along to the polls like everyone else. But once turnout drops, as so often happens in second-order elections, young people are then the most likely to be left on the political sidelines these days.

TABLE 4.10

Percent Reporting Casting a Ballot by Age Categories for the European Parliament, 1979 and 1999

	18–29	30–44	45–64	65+	OLDEST/YOUNGEST RATIO
FRANCE 1979	46	69	71	73	1.6 : 1
FRANCE 1999	42	51	67	72	1.7 : 1
NETHERLANDS 1979	59	67	78	77	1.3 : 1
NETHERLANDS 1999	42	44	56	70	1.7 : 1
WEST GERMANY 1979	69	74	71	67	1.0 : 1
WEST GERMANY 1999	40	54	61	59	1.5 : 1
ITALY 1979	94	96	97	95	1.0 : 1
ITALY 1999	79	84	84	81	1.0 : 1
DENMARK 1979	62	68	74	69	1.1 : 1
DENMARK 1999	57	69	79	72	1.3 : 1
IRELAND 1979	71	80	87	79	1.1 : 1
IRELAND 1999	39	70	83	72	1.8 : 1
GREAT BRITAIN 1979	41	51	62	63	1.5 : 1
GREAT BRITAIN 1999	18	27	37	50	2.8 : 1

Source: Eurobarometers, 1979 and 1999.

CONCLUSION: WAS LOWERING THE VOTING AGE A MISTAKE?

Considering how little use young adults have made of the voting franchise in recent years, some might consider the action of lowering the voting age to 18 in most established democracies to have been a mistake. This point of view is well expressed by political scientist Mark Franklin, who writes that:

> *With the benefit of hindsight, this reform was a really bad idea. It turns out that the well-intentioned decision to enfranchise young adults one election earlier than previously had the unanticipated consequence of giving rise to a lifetime of disenfranchisement for many of the intended beneficiaries. Ironically, almost any other age from fifteen to twenty-five would be a better age for individuals to first be confronted with the need to acquire the skills and knowledge necessary for casting a vote.*[72]

Franklin's argument here is based on the quite sensible premise that both voting and nonvoting are habits, and that if someone doesn't participate in his or her first election, then a lifetime habit of nonvoting may well be the result.

Though this theory regarding turnout decline seems sound at first glance, it doesn't hold up too well empirically. A number of findings presented in this chapter indicate that it would be a mistake to blame the recent decline of turnout in many countries on the lowering of the voting age. The cross-national data do *not* support the notion of an immutable life cycle effect in which the turnout of newly enfranchised voters will necessarily be rather low. Indeed, in the early 1970s most countries had no real problem in getting young people to vote—even after many countries had lowered the voting age to 18. And the only established democracy that still does not allow 18- and 19-year-olds to vote—Japan—has nevertheless seen turnout decline sharply and a wide generation gap in electoral participation develop.

The central reason that so many of today's young adults fail to vote is not the age they are at but rather their lack of exposure to politics. Mark Franklin is certainly right to point to the problem of a lack of political skills among newly eligible voters these days. However, the data presented in previous chapters of this book indicate that this has not always been the case—including when most countries lowered the voting age. No one at that time could have foreseen that young adults in the twenty-first century would have such low levels of newspaper reading, TV news watching, or political knowledge.

Such trends lead me to be very skeptical regarding the current reform proposed in some circles to further lower the voting age to 16.[73] Based on an analysis of survey data from the European Social Survey, which includes 16- and 17-year-olds, this age group is presently even less likely to follow political news than people just a few years older.[74] Of course, if young people were given the franchise and required by high school teachers to follow politics as part of their classwork, this state of affairs could well change. But it seems risky to count on such assignments having a long-term impact on the media habits of young people.

It would perhaps be more likely for teachers to instill a stronger sense of the civic duty to vote if young people were confronted with the task of voting while they are in high school. Whether or not the voting age is lowered, this is certainly a goal that teachers need to address, as the data in the following chapter will demonstrate.

CHAPTER 5

Do Young Adults See
Voting as a Civic Duty?

Besides caring about who wins, another common reason political scientists have found for why some people vote is that they believe it is their civic duty. As Angus Campbell et al. wrote in their classic 1960 book *The American Voter*, "Wide currency in American society is given the idea that the individual has a civic responsibility to vote. When this norm becomes a part of the value system of the individual, as it has for most of our citizens, it may be regarded as a force acting directly on the turnout decision."[75] Andre Blais goes even further, arguing that many people who feel a duty to vote do so out of a sense of moral obligation. He writes, "To use a religious analogy, not voting can be construed as a venial sin: it is a wrong, one that weak human beings should be urged not to commit but may be forgiven for if they indulge in it."[76]

How one's sense of civic duty can influence the decision whether to vote or not was driven home to me in a very personal way in November 1998. I must confess that I did not vote in that election. Like many fellow baby boomers, I was relatively nonchalant about failing to participate. In my own mind, I felt that I had a pretty good excuse: About a week before the election, my father had undergone heart bypass surgery. I had flown across the country on short notice to be there, and the thought of getting an absentee ballot before I left California was not something that crossed my mind. (By the time I arrived on the East Coast, it was too late to request an absentee ballot by mail, but I later realized that I could have requested one in person just before I had left.) Ironically, I was able to keep a few commitments on election day to do radio interviews on the topic of nonvoting by simply e-mailing the producers that I would be at a different phone number. The fact that I wasn't voting that day came up a couple times on the air and led to some interesting discussions, but no real embarrassment on my part.

My father, by contrast, took a very different view regarding not voting. He had just gotten out of the hospital a couple days before election day and had scarcely been able to walk 10 yards outside the house, but nevertheless he said on Tuesday morning that he wanted to be driven to the polls. This idea did not sound wise to me under the circumstances. I proposed an alternative: given that my parents were clearly going to vote for different candidates for governor, I suggested that neither one vote, rather than go to the trouble of canceling out one another. This suggestion met with sharp resistance from my mother, who reminded me that there were many offices on the ballot besides governor and that they might actually agree on some of them. Most importantly, both my parents said that they considered it their duty as citizens to vote. My father pointedly remarked that voting was something that people who are alive are supposed to do, and having just survived a difficult, major surgery, he was absolutely determined to act as one who is alive. Facing such adamant demands, I felt little choice but to find some way to get my parents to the polls, and indeed went to more trouble to ensure that they voted than I would to cast a ballot myself.[77]

My parents' insistence that they really wanted to vote, my casual baby boomer attitude toward voting, and the outright political apathy I frequently see among today's college students are apparently all representative of current generational attitudes regarding the duty to vote. The goal of this chapter is to flesh out how these generational differences have emerged, both in the United States and in other established democracies.

HAVE YOUNG AMERICANS BECOME LESS LIKELY TO VIEW VOTING AS A DUTY?

Campbell et al. called voting a "responsibility" and Blais termed it an "obligation." To what extent do young people in the United States agree with such views? A 2002 CIRCLE survey of 1200 Americans between the ages of 15 and 25 provides some insight. This survey posed the following question: "In your mind, which word best describes how you feel about voting: a right, a responsibility, a choice, or a duty?" Twenty percent responded that they considered voting a responsibility, and 9 percent said they felt it was a duty. Thus, less than one out of three young Americans expressed a view of voting as a civic obligation. On the other side of the coin, 34 percent responded that voting was a choice and another 31 percent called it a right.[78] It would be reading too much into such responses to say that these two-thirds of young Americans didn't value voting; they could well have seen voting as a fundamental right or a crucial choice. Nevertheless, without a strong sense that electoral participation is a responsibility and a duty for everyone, it seems reasonable to conclude that many of these young adults will not vote on a regular basis.

Whether young people are currently less likely than older adults to view voting as a civic duty remains to be established. Unfortunately, CIRCLE's interesting question has not been posed to a national sample of all ages. The best questions I'm aware of in any recent survey on the topic of voting as a civic duty are two that were asked by the Pew Research Center in their June 2000 and August 2003 surveys. Over 8500 randomly selected individuals were asked whether they agreed with the statements "I feel it's my duty as a citizen to always vote" and "I feel guilty when I don't get a chance to vote." Overall, 63 percent completely agreed with the notion that it is one's duty to vote—roughly the same percentage of citizens who voted in 2004. And 37 percent said they feel guilty if they don't vote—roughly the same percentage of people who voted in the midterm election of 1998 that my father was so determined to participate in. As can be seen in the data displayed in Table 5.1, senior citizens were 1.7 times more likely than people under the age of 30 to completely agree that it is one's duty to vote, and 1.8 times as likely to say they feel guilty if they don't vote.

It might be argued that such age patterns are nothing to worry about, because one's sense of civic responsibility will increase as one grows older. Indeed, Andre Blais writes that "people are more likely to construe voting as a citizen duty as they grow older. On

TABLE 5.1

Percent Completely Agreeing in Recent Years with Statements
Regarding the Duty to Vote

	18–29	30–44	45–64	65+
"I FEEL IT'S MY DUTY AS A CITIZEN TO ALWAYS VOTE."	44	61	71	75
"I FEEL GUILTY WHEN I DON'T GET A CHANCE TO VOTE."	24	34	44	44

Source: June 2000 and August 2003 Pew Research Center surveys.

the one hand, their sense of attachment to their community increases, which makes them more inclined to think about duties toward the community. On the other hand, they have more exposure to the dominant norm that the good citizen ought to vote."[79] Although the factors that Blais lists seem sensible, he offers no supporting data; we should thus not presume that his hunch is correct, especially considering that some countervailing factors can also be hypothesized. Firstly, the concept of voting as a civic duty is taught in school, and lessons learned in school may be gradually forgotten if they don't prove relevant in later life. Many people quickly forget the algebra and chemistry they learned; why wouldn't they also forget concepts from civics courses? Secondly, as Americans grow older they are likely to see that many of their friends, relatives, and neighbors don't vote and that the political system continues to thrive anyway. Such life experiences may well lead some people to question whether it really is one's duty to vote.

The landmark socialization study of the high school class of 1965 and their parents provides some telling data indicating that students were substantially more likely than their parents to mention participation in politics as one of the most important qualities of good citizenship. Jennings and Niemi noted this difference and attributed it to "years of repetitious schoolroom exhortation to participate" that the high school students had received.[80] In their follow-up study, based on reinterviews eight years later, the impact of these exhortations was found to have worn off considerably, leading Jennings and Niemi to note that "As one enters the adult world, the difficulty of living up to these prescriptions becomes more obvious."[81]

Since the original 1965–1973 panel study, both generations were reinterviewed for a third time in 1982, and, incredibly, many respondents from the class of 1965 participated in a fourth interview in 1997.[82] One can hardly imagine a better source of data to test a life cycle hypothesis than these interviews with the same individuals over so many years. Table 5.2 traces the frequency over time with which those interviewed mentioned political participation as an important attribute of a good citizen. Rather than a life cycle, the data mostly

TABLE 5.2
Percent of Panel Respondents Who Mentioned Political Participation as an Important Attribute of a Good Citizen, 1965–1997

	1965	1973	1982	1997
CLASS OF 1965 HIGH SCHOOL SENIORS	70	57	54	52
PARENTS OF THE CLASS OF 1965	48	40	44	—

Question wording: "People have different ideas about what being a good citizen means. Tell me how you would describe a good citizen in this country—that is, what things about a person are most important in showing that he is a good citizen?" Up to four responses coded. Codes 20 through 29 were counted as involving political participation.

Source: Youth-Parent Socialization Panel Study.

point to the stability of such attitudes over one's lifetime. Once the immediate effects of their schooling had worn off, there is relatively little change evident in the younger generation's responses between the ages of 25 and 50. Similarly, their parents' responses were similar in all three waves, with feelings of civic duty consistently being somewhat less salient for them than for their offspring.

Because feelings of civic duty are apparently established early in one's adult life and remain fairly stable afterward, it is important to continually reexamine age patterns, as the entrance of new cohorts into the population may well change the overall picture. The limited time series data available from the U.S. National Election Studies would indicate that the relationship between age and civic duty has indeed changed over the years. Over the course of five decades, these surveys have periodically asked respondents whether they agree or disagree with the following statement: "So many other people vote in the national elections that it doesn't matter much to me whether I vote or not." As can be seen in Table 5.3, in recent

TABLE 5.3
Percent Expressing a Sense of Citizen Duty by Age in the United States, 1952–2002

	<30	30–44	45–64	65+	DIFFERENCE BETWEEN 65+ AND <30
1952–1960	91	92	90	85	−6
1972–1980	87	91	92	87	0
2000–2002	70	82	86	80	+10

Question wording: "So many other people vote in the national elections that it doesn't matter much to me whether I vote or not." Table entries represent the percentage who disagreed with the statement.

Source: U.S. National Election Studies, 1952–2002. (not asked in 2004)

years it has been young Americans who have been the *least* likely to express a clear sense of civic duty by disagreeing with the statement. In contrast, in the 1972–1980 period there was no clear age pattern, and in the very early years of the election studies, the elderly were slightly less likely than other age groups to indicate that voting really did matter to them.

In sum, the fact that today's young Americans are the least likely to view voting as a civic duty is troubling in a number of respects. Contrary to any notion of a life cycle effect, it has not always been the case that young people possess the weakest sense of citizen duty with regard to voting. Rather, this is something new. Furthermore, panel data collected over time indicate that we cannot necessarily expect young people's attitudes on the duties of citizenship to change as they age.

Of course, such conclusions must be viewed with some caution, given that they are based on relatively limited data. Data from other countries regarding citizen duty provide crucial confirmation of these American findings.

CAN SIMILAR TRENDS BE FOUND IN OTHER DEMOCRACIES?

The scholars who designed the first major cross-national surveys were very concerned with the question of how people viewed the responsibilities of citizenship. The famous Civic Culture Study by Almond and Verba posed an open-ended question that asked respondents what obligations citizens owed their country. Similar questions (some open-ended and some closed-ended) were asked in the follow-up Participation and Political Equality Study a decade later.

Table 5.4 presents data regarding the frequency with which respondents of different age groups said that political participation was an important citizen duty. In the five countries where an open-ended question was asked, there were wide differences in

TABLE 5.4
Percent Saying that Political Participation Is a Very Important Citizen Obligation, 1959–1970

	<30	30–44	45–64	65+	DIFFERENCE BETWEEN 65+ AND <30
OPEN-ENDED QUESTION					
GREAT BRITAIN 1959	7	5	7	6	−1
GERMANY 1959	39	35	33	35	−4
ITALY 1959	6	7	7	2	−4
USA 1960	44	43	37	30	−14
USA 1967	53	54	43	36	−17
JAPAN 1967	12	11	7	4	−8
CLOSED-ENDED QUESTION					
AUSTRIA 1967	73	63	57	47	−26
NETHERLANDS 1970	70	70	70	60	−10

Open-ended question wording: 1959 & 1960–"People speak of the obligations which they owe to their country. In your opinion what are the obligations which every man owes his country?"; USA 1967–"What do you think is the most important obligation a citizen has to his country?"; Japan 1967–"What are the most important duties of a citizen?"

Closed-ended question wording: Austria 1967–"Here is a list of duties that it may be necessary for citizens to perform for a nation to continue. Which do you think is most important: work hard, be active in politics, obey the laws, be informed about public problems?" (% choosing be active in politics or be informed about public problems as one of their choices reported in the table); Netherlands 1970–"Do you think that a citizen should play a very active role in public life, or rather active, or do you think this is not necessary?" (% saying very or rather reported in the table).

Sources: Civic Culture Study, 1959–1960; Participation and Political Equality Study, 1967–1970.

terms of how likely people were to mention political participation. In Germany and the United States, over a third of respondents spontaneously said something along the lines of voting, keeping informed about politics, or expressing one's political views. In contrast, less than 10 percent said something along these lines in Great Britain, Italy, and Japan. (The most common responses in these countries were as follows: Great Britain—to do one's job right; Italy—to be moral and honest; Japan—to pay taxes.) Despite these disparities, the age patterns are consistent in all five countries, either with little difference between age categories or with young people being slightly more likely to mention political participation as an important citizen obligation.

More direct measures of the concept of political obligation can be found in some closed-ended questions that were asked in Austria in 1967 and the Netherlands in 1970. In Austria, the younger someone was, the more likely he or she was to choose either being active in politics or being informed about public problems from among a list of important citizen duties. And in the Netherlands, both young and middle-aged respondents were more likely than the elderly to think that citizens should play a rather active role in public life. Thus, both open-ended and closed-ended survey data indicate that young adults in established democracies had a relatively strong sense of citizen duty during the 1959–1970 era.

Recent survey data from a wide spectrum of countries reveal that young adults in the twenty-first century are far different in this respect. Table 5.5 displays data from 15 established democracies regarding the percentage within each age group who expressed a strong sense that it is a citizen's duty to vote. In all

TABLE 5.5

Percentage of Respondents in Various Countries Expressing a Strong Sense that it Is a Citizen's Duty to Vote, Circa 2002

	18–29	30–44	45–64	65+	DIFFERENCE BETWEEN 65+ AND <30
FINLAND	24	35	51	63	+39
GREAT BRITAIN	23	29	45	59	+36
NEW ZEALAND	28	40	48	61	+33
CANADA	55	74	80	85	+30
JAPAN	32	44	64	61	+29
DENMARK	54	66	78	82	+28
NORWAY	37	51	49	60	+23
GERMANY	36	40	48	58	+22
IRELAND	35	44	53	57	+22
SWITZERLAND	30	31	37	49	+19
AUSTRIA	44	53	63	62	+18
NETHERLANDS	26	32	39	44	+18
SWEDEN	56	55	62	72	+16
FRANCE	51	51	67	65	+14
ITALY	30	41	48	42	+12

Question wording: Europe—"To be a good citizen, how important would you say it is for a person to vote in elections: 0 = extremely unimportant; 10 = extremely important." (percent responding 9 or 10 shown in the table); Japan—"Many people vote at elections, so it doesn't matter if I don't." (percent clearly disagreeing shown in the table); New Zealand—"It is a citizen's duty to vote." (percent strongly agreeing shown in the table); Canada—"It is every citizen's duty to vote in federal elections." (percent strongly agreeing shown in the table).

Sources: European Social Survey, 2002/3; 2000 Japanese Social Survey; 2002 New Zealand Election Study; 2004 Canadian Election Study.

15 countries, a clear relationship between age and feelings of citizen duty is readily apparent, with young adults being considerably less likely than their elders to say that voting is an extremely important quality of good citizenship.

Tellingly, the countries that have the biggest generation gaps in terms of turnout, such as Great Britain and Japan, generally also have the largest age differences in opinion regarding the duty to vote. The correlation between the two age-difference measures is fairly strong, .56 (p < .05). Thus, one of the reasons for the decline of youth turnout in so many established democracies is no doubt the relative lack among today's young people of a sense of a civic obligation to vote.

CONCLUSION: A WINDOW INTO THE FUTURE?

Besides providing insight into turnout problems in these countries today, attitudes concerning civic duty among recent entrants into the electorate may well provide a window into the future. Because the current generation of young people has a relatively weak sense of citizen duty, its current poor turnout rates may well be a constant state of affairs throughout their lifetimes. A generation who is relatively unlikely to see voting as an important civic responsibility is one who may well have many of its members lost as voters for the rest of its duration.

Short of implementing compulsory voting, which we will discuss in the final chapter, it is probably too late to convince people who have already entered early adulthood that it is their obligation as citizens to vote. But it is never too late to convince people that politics really matters. One way to do this is to illustrate that, by passing up opportunities to vote, they are ceding important decisions to others who have different values and interests. As will be seen in the next chapter, young people are indeed doing just that.

CHAPTER 6

Does Low Youth Turnout
Really Matter?

Although much research has been done on the topic of nonvoting, there is a surprising lack of concern among scholars about its consequences. This is not to say that scholars don't care if everyone votes or not. Implicit in most studies of voter turnout is a generally accepted norm that in an ideal democracy, all adult citizens vote in all elections. The fact that most democracies fall far short of this ideal does not trouble many scholars because they judge the results of elections to be largely unbiased by who votes and who does not. Wolfinger and Rosenstone's classic book *Who Votes?* demonstrates that nonvoters are demographically different from voters, but argues that "these demographic biases do not translate into discernible overrepresentation of particular policy constituencies."[83] Ruy Teixeira's excellent book on the decline of U.S. turnout asks the question of "What if they gave an election and everybody came?" and arrives at an answer of "Not much."[84]

He also places much weight on the finding that demographic factors are not related to policy preferences closely enough to result in substantial differences in the political attitudes of voters and nonvoters. Most recently, Verba, Schlozman, and Brady say in their comprehensive review of participation in the United States that "our data support the conclusion that voters and non-voters do not seem to differ substantially in their attitudes on public policy issues."[85] In effect, these scholars have posed the question of "Why worry about disappointing electoral participation rates given that there is little difference between voters and nonvoters in terms of political behavior?"

The answer of this book is that whenever young adults are substantially less likely to vote than their elders, the ideal of government of the people, by the people, and for the people is seriously compromised. Most importantly, a democratically elected government should be looking out *for* the interests of *all* the people. If politicians know that young people are far less likely to vote than the elderly, why should they care about young people?

Officeholders need to concern themselves with their *core constituency*—the people who put them in power in the first place, and whose support they'll need to get reelected. According to David Mayhew, most politicians place reelection as their highest goal, and in order to reach it they engage in advertising and credit claiming aimed at their primary constituency.[86] From the perspective of this book, this means that politicians will be more likely to do something that will earn them credit with the elderly than with young adults. Thus, if there is a choice between passing legislation to reduce either the costs of prescription drugs or college education, the reelection imperative will naturally bias politicians to focus their energies on the former.

As John Kingdon has shown, the process by which some problems more than others come to occupy the attention of governmental officials is an important key to understanding what the government actually does.[87] Part of that process involves rational calculations by politicians regarding who is likely to vote and who is not. If young adults don't vote, then the issues that most concern them will often fail to make it onto the political agenda.

This chapter demonstrates that the concerns of young adults are indeed quite distinct from those of their elders. These divergent concerns translate into differences on the ideological spectrum and on various policy issues. Furthermore, evidence from recent U.S. elections, as well as elections from other established democracies, indicates that *more young people voting would definitely make a difference because the youth vote often favors different candidates and parties.*

DOES POSITION IN THE LIFE CYCLE AFFECT POLICY POSITIONS?

Winston Churchill is said to have remarked that "Any man who is not a socialist at the age of 21 has no heart, and any man who is still a socialist at the age of 40 has no head." The first part of the quote can be taken as saying that it is easy to favor economic equality when one is a young adult in the process of getting educated, finding a job, and beginning a career. But the second part implies that the notion of equality of income for all looks far different once one is middle aged and established in an occupation. In short, what the quote illuminates is that where one stands on the issues of the day depends in part on where one stands in life. An individual's place in the life cycle plays an important role in determining the kind of personal experiences that seem relevant at any given point in time, which in turn affects one's political priorities and values.

A Pew Research Center survey from October 2004 allows us to quantify the degree to which age differences exist on a variety of experiences that may have some political relevance. The findings displayed in Table 6.1 largely confirm commonsense expectations but are nevertheless instructive. Young adults by far are the most likely to be facing the challenges of paying for a college education and finding a job. On the other side of the coin, they are the least likely to own a small business or trade stocks and bonds. These economic experiences (or lack thereof) should make young people more likely to support activist policies of governmental intervention in the economy and to be less supportive of a probusiness policy agenda. Additionally, young people have a notably different lifestyle from the elderly on three key aspects of the new Right agenda. They are 1) less inclined to be a born-again or evangelical Christian; 2) more likely to have a friend, colleague, or family member who is gay; and 3) less likely to have a gun or rifle at home.

Based on these findings, one would expect that young adults in the United States should be substantially more liberal than older people. Because this expectation stems from young people's position in the life cycle, such a pattern should be consistent at various points in time. Yet, it should also be the case that as people progress from young adulthood to middle age, they will turn more conservative.

TABLE 6.1

Lifestyle Differences by Age (percent responding affirmatively)

	18–29	30–44	45–64	65+
DO YOU HAVE A FRIEND, COLLEAGUE, OR FAMILY MEMBER WHO IS CURRENTLY SERVING IN THE MILITARY, RESERVES, OR NATIONAL GUARD?	67	61	53	40
DO YOU HAPPEN TO HAVE ANY GUNS, RIFLES, OR PISTOLS IN YOUR HOME?	31	35	45	44
ARE YOU THE OWNER OF A SMALL BUSINESS?	6	22	18	9
DO YOU TRADE STOCKS OR BONDS IN THE STOCK MARKET?	14	36	40	27
OVER THE PAST 12 MONTHS, HAS THERE BEEN A TIME WHEN YOU OR SOMEONE IN YOUR HOUSEHOLD HAS BEEN WITHOUT A JOB AND LOOKING FOR WORK, OR NOT?	48	38	36	21
OVER THE PAST 12 MONTHS, HAS THERE BEEN A TIME WHEN YOU HAVE BEEN UNABLE TO AFFORD NECESSARY HEALTH CARE FOR YOURSELF OR A FAMILY MEMBER, OR NOT?	22	30	27	16
ARE YOU CURRENTLY PAYING FOR THE COSTS OF COLLEGE TUITION OR STUDENT LOANS FOR YOURSELF OR SOMEONE IN YOUR FAMILY?	44	30	23	9
DO YOU HAVE A FRIEND, COLLEAGUE, OR FAMILY MEMBER WHO IS GAY?	49	52	48	25
WOULD YOU DESCRIBE YOURSELF AS A "BORN AGAIN" OR EVANGELICAL CHRISTIAN, OR NOT?	29	32	34	37

Source: October 2004 Pew Research Center survey.

All of these expectations are confirmed by the 1972–2004 General Social Surveys data presented in Table 6.2. The data collected in the early twenty-first century reveal that among people born in the 1980s, there are substantially more liberals than conservatives,

TABLE 6.2

Cohort Analysis of Political Ideology, 1972–2004
[entries are % conservative − % liberal]

BORN IN:	2000–2004	1990s	1980s	1970s
1980s	−14			
1970s	+1	−5		
1960s	+11	+4	−1	
1950s	+9	+5	−4	−21
1940s	+13	+8	+5	−9
1930s	+24	+19	+16	+13
1920s	+17	+20	+18	+15
1910s		+18	+14	+14

Source: General Social Surveys, 1972–2004.

whereas just the opposite is the case among those born in the 1920s and 1930s.[88] Interestingly, the latter group grew up during the height of liberalism when New Deal policies advocated by Presidents Franklin Roosevelt and Harry Truman reshaped the nation. The fact that this generation of New Dealers is now a mainstay of conservatism supports the theory that people move away from liberalism as they age. Indeed, there is clear evidence of a rightward shift of opinion among all the cohorts whose ideology we can track for decades, starting from a relatively young age. Americans like myself born in the 1950s provide a perfect example: Children of the 1950s were clearly quite liberal in the 1970s; by the 1980s their liberalism had moderated; as of the 1990s they were more likely to be conservatives than liberals; and in the twenty-first century their conservative tendencies have increased further.

To more fully understand why political conservatism increases with age, it is helpful to look at a wide range of specific issues. The 2000 National Annenberg Election Study is particularly useful for examining age differences on issues because it has such a large sample size (over 94,000) and because over the course of the year many issues were asked about. Table 6.3 displays data from this survey on a wide range of issues that elicited a clear generation gap. As expected based on their economic stage in life, young people are the most supportive of government policies that will

TABLE 6.3
Age Differences on Public Policy Issues in 2000

	18–29	30–44	45–64	65+
LIBERAL	31	23	21	16
MODERATE	39	41	40	39
CONSERVATIVE	29	36	39	45
FAVOR GOVERNMENT POLICIES TO REDUCE INCOME DIFFERENCES	61	53	46	42
SPEND MORE MONEY ON MILITARY	35	42	54	65
SPEND MORE MONEY ON EDUCATION	81	74	62	53
SPEND MORE MONEY ON AID TO MOTHERS WITH YOUNG CHILDREN	59	49	43	43
SPEND MORE MONEY ON SOCIAL SECURITY	61	60	59	50
FAVOR INVESTING SOCIAL SECURITY IN STOCK MARKET	71	68	60	45
FAVOR SCHOOL VOUCHERS	44	40	35	30
FAVOR GAYS IN MILITARY	64	62	59	53
GOVERNMENT SHOULD DO MORE TO PROTECT THE ENVIRONMENT	77	69	62	59

Source: 2000 National Annenberg Election Study.

reduce income differences. Specifically, they are naturally more in favor of increased government spending on items such as education and aid to mothers with young children. But the biggest generational gap on spending priorities is on the military budget, with only about a third of young adults favoring more spending for American armed forces and weaponry compared to two-thirds of senior citizens. Young people thus seem to realize the trade-off between social services spending and defense spending, with a clear preference for the former. Interestingly, their preference for more social services applies even to something that most of them believe they will never benefit from—Social Security.

Young Americans do not reject every conservative idea out of hand, however. When it comes to President Bush's proposal to allow people to invest some of their Social Security contributions in the stock market, young adults are by far the most supportive age group. In addition, they are substantially more in favor of the conservative-backed proposal for school vouchers that would enable parents to receive public funds to send their children to private schools. What these two examples illustrate is that young people are the most open to new ideas, regardless of the ideas' ideological origins. Indeed, on two relatively new liberal ideas—gay rights and government action to protect the environment—young people are also the most in agreement.

Perhaps surprisingly given that young adults bear the physical risks of waging war, their willingness to embrace new policy endeavors applies to foreign commitments of American military might as well. When asked whether we did the right thing going into Iraq, Pew Research Center surveys in 2003, 2004, and 2005 consistently found young adults to be more approving of the war than senior citizens were. It might be thought that such an age pattern is due to the unique circumstance of America's now living under the threat of terrorist attacks. Yet, as Table 6.4 demonstrates, young people were also the most likely to say that we had done the right thing in getting into Korea and Vietnam.

Today, many antiwar activists yearn for the spirit of protest seen during the 1960s, when many of America's youth spoke up loud and clear in opposition to the Vietnam War. The lack of a very vocal opposition to the Iraq War among today's youth is sometimes seen as yet another indicator of their seeming political apathy. These

TABLE 6.4
Percent Saying We Did the Right Thing Getting into Various Wars by Age Group

	18–29	30–44	45–64	65+
KOREA 1952	55	48	37	29
VIETNAM 1964	59	55	42	31
VIETNAM 1966	56	55	44	35
VIETNAM 1968	39	40	25	19
VIETNAM 1970	42	38	26	16
VIETNAM 1972	36	38	27	16
IRAQ JULY 2003	66	67	63	54
IRAQ SEPTEMBER 2004	59	56	53	42
IRAQ JULY 2005	55	53	47	37

Question wording: Korea: "Do you think we did the right thing in getting into the fighting in Korea two years ago or should we have stayed out?"; Vietnam: "Do you think we did the right thing in getting into the fighting in Vietnam or should we have stayed out?"; Iraq: "Do you think the U.S. made the right decision or the wrong decision in using military force against Iraq?"

Source: 1952–1972 American National Election Studies; 2003–2005 Pew Research Center surveys.

stereotypes are clearly exaggerated, however. The survey data from both eras reveal that young Americans supported the war more than their elders did. Ultimately, going to war in a democracy involves trusting the judgment of the country's leaders that the cause justifies the sacrifices. Just as young Americans are known to be more generally trusting of government, so are they also apparently more likely to say that their government is doing the right thing in going to war.

Once the Vietnam War turned unpopular overall, it was naturally the young people who turned out to demonstrate, as throughout world history taking to the barricades has been the province of youth. Should the Iraq War turn equally unpopular, demanding sacrifices from the country that appear unjustified, then antiwar activities are likely to pick up again among young Americans. When George W. Bush ran for reelection in 2004, such a state of affairs did not exist, as evidenced by the fact that Democratic nominee John Kerry had voted for the war and continually said that the country needed to keep its troops in Iraq. Young people thus had many policy reasons for being more against President Bush than other age groups were in 2004, but the Iraq War was not prominent among them.

IS THERE A GENERATION GAP IN AMERICAN VOTING BEHAVIOR?

From these various data, two hypotheses can be drawn concerning the types of candidates whom young Americans should be particularly inclined to support. First, because of their openness to new policy approaches, they should be more susceptible to the appeals of third-party candidates. Second, given that their policy stands are generally more in line with liberal principles than are their elders', they should be more likely to have supported the Democrats in recent elections.

Having grown up with multiple choices in virtually every aspect of American life, today's young adults should be particularly likely to want more choices in the political arena. Young adults would hardly be content with having a choice between just Coke and Pepsi given all the choices they have become accustomed to. The same is true for the choice between Democrats and Republicans. In the 2000 U.S. National Election Study, respondents were asked which of the following outcomes regarding political parties best represented what they would like to see happen—a continuation of the two-party system, elections in which candidates run as individuals without party labels, or the growth of one or more parties that could effectively challenge the Democrats and Republicans. People under the age of 30 were the least supportive of the political status quo, with only 28 percent saying they wanted to retain the current two-party system, as compared to 55 percent of senior citizens. Young adults were more in favor of both candidates running without party labels—as Ross Perot did in 1992—and the development of a viable third party.

Such attitudes have been regularly translated into votes for presidential candidates running outside the two-party system. As can be seen from Table 6.5, in every case where a significant independent or third-party candidate emerged, young voters were the most likely to cast their ballots for him. Notably, this age pattern occurred regardless of the ideology of the insurgent contender. Young voters were the most supportive of liberals Ralph Nader and John Anderson, centrist Ross Perot, and conservative George Wallace alike. These results should not be taken as indicating that

TABLE 6.5

Percent Voting for Prominent Independent/Third-Party Candidates
for President, 1968–2000

	18–29	30–44	45–64	65+
GEORGE WALLACE 1968	15	11	12	8
JOHN ANDERSON 1980	16	11	8	3
ROSS PEROT 1992	28	19	17	12
ROSS PEROT 1996	14	11	7	5
RALPH NADER 2000	5	2	2	2

Sources: 1968, 1980, 1992, and 1996 National Election Studies; 2000 National Voter
Exit Poll.

young adults in recent years have had no ideological anchoring.
Rather, what is operative in each case is that young people have felt
less tied to the *traditional* ideological choices. When conservative
third-party candidates appear, they can expect to get disproportionate support from young conservatives, and liberal third-party
candidates can expect to get disproportionate support from young
liberals. Were more young people to turn out at the polls, it is likely
that more prominent individuals would challenge the two-party
system, knowing that more voters would be open to their appeals.
Thus, the lack of young voters at the polls really does matter in
that it helps perpetuate America's two-party system. Some will
see this effect as a good thing, whereas others will see it as
unfortunate; but everyone should agree that it is consequential.

The extraordinary closeness of the 2000 and 2004 presidential
elections has made it clearer than ever before in recent memory
that who votes can make a big difference. A variety of changes in
group turnout rates in the key states of Florida in 2000 and Ohio

TABLE 6.6
Percent Voting for George W. Bush by Age in Key States

	18–29	30–44	45–64	65+
2000 FLORIDA	40	51	49	52
2004 OHIO	42	52	52	58

Source: Voter News Service Exit Polls.

in 2004 could have swung the outcome in favor of the Democrats in both cases. In particular, if more young people had voted, there is good reason to believe that George W. Bush would *not* have won. As can be seen from the exit poll data displayed in Table 6.6, only 40 percent of Floridians under the age of 30 cast their ballots for Bush in 2000 compared to 52 percent among senior citizens. Given the razor-thin margin of victory, it is readily apparent that if turnout rates among young people had been just slightly higher, Gore would have carried the state, and hence won the White House. If turnout rates had been equal across generations, and if nonvoters had voted like actual participants of the same age,[89] Gore's share of the two-party vote would have been approximately 50.8 percent, thereby making a recount unnecessary. Four years later in the key state of Ohio, the generation gap was even greater, with 42 percent of the youngest voters supporting Bush compared to 58 percent of seniors. In this case, if all age groups had voted at the same rate, Bush's narrow 51.1 percent of the two-party vote would have been transformed into a dead heat requiring a recount. In short, the low turnout rate of young adults in 2000 and 2004 really mattered, denying crucial votes to Al Gore and John Kerry that could have changed the course of history.

Are There Age Gaps in Ideology and
Voting Behavior in Other Countries?

Further evidence that low turnout among young adults really makes a difference can be found by examining recent survey data from other established democracies. If, as Churchill said, socialism looks a lot better to young people, then there should be a relationship between age and ideology where socialist principles have long been instrumental in defining the ideological spectrum, such as in most of Europe. In addition, young people are more in tune with post-material concerns such as the environment, which have increasingly come to shape left-wing thought in many established democracies.[90] The data on average ideological self-placement by age group displayed in Table 6.7 confirm these expectations. In 16 of the 18 countries, young adults are substantially more likely to place themselves to the left than older people.

Interestingly, the countries that have the sharpest age differences on ideology are also where the turnout disparity between young and old is most pronounced. In other words, not only are young Japanese, British, Irish, and New Zealand adults particularly less likely to vote compared to their grandparents' generation, but they are also substantially less right-wing. Austrian, Swedish, and Italian youth, by contrast, are fairly similar to their elders in both turnout rates and ideology. The correlation between the two difference measures is a striking .72, far too great to be due to chance (p < .001).[91] Correlation does not necessarily imply causation, and there is no clear answer to the question of why these two phenomena are related. It may be that when young people feel differently from older people on the issues, the choices offered by the parties lack an appeal to the young. In contrast,

TABLE 6.7
Left-Right Positioning by Age in Established Democracies, Circa 2000

	<30	30-44	45-64	65+	DIFFERENCE BETWEEN 65+ AND <30
JAPAN	5.0	5.4	6.0	6.1	+1.1
GREAT BRITAIN	4.8	4.9	5.0	5.7	+0.9
IRELAND	5.2	5.5	5.8	6.1	+0.9
NEW ZEALAND	5.1	5.9	5.8	6.0	+0.9
AUSTRALIA	5.0	5.2	5.6	5.7	+0.7
CANADA	5.2	5.6	5.6	5.9	+0.7
SWITZERLAND	5.1	5.1	5.4	5.8	+0.7
USA	5.6	5.7	5.8	6.3	+0.7
FINLAND	5.7	5.6	5.8	6.2	+0.5
BELGIUM	5.1	5.1	5.4	5.5	+0.4
DENMARK	5.6	5.4	5.3	6.0	+0.4
FRANCE	4.7	4.6	5.1	5.1	+0.4
GERMANY	5.6	5.4	5.3	6.0	+0.4
NETHERLANDS	5.1	4.9	5.0	5.5	+0.4
NORWAY	5.5	5.4	5.7	5.9	+0.4
ITALY	5.4	5.3	5.2	5.7	+0.3
AUSTRIA	5.3	5.3	5.4	5.4	+0.1
SWEDEN	5.3	5.3	5.3	5.4	+0.1

Question wording: "In political matters, people talk of 'left' and 'right.' How would you place your views on this scale, generally speaking?" 1 = Left; 10 = Right

Source: 1999–2001 World Values Study.

where there are few ideological differences between generations, the same appeals can mobilize all age groups to go to the polls. In any event, the very existence of this relationship certainly implies that low youth turnout matters. In countries where young people's turnout rates are well below average, their views are not likely to be well represented at the polls by their elders who do vote.

Indeed, there are sizable age differences in voting behavior in these countries. Table 6.8 presents survey data on voting choices by age for the countries where there is a considerable generation gap in electoral participation. In order to streamline the presentation, only parties for which there was at least a 5-percentage-point difference in support between the youngest and oldest voters are shown in the table. For example, voting for the British Labour Party in 2005 is not shown because there were only slight differences by age group, whereas young people were clearly more likely to vote for the Liberal Democrats and less inclined to support the Conservatives. In Canada, age differences are found across the partisan spectrum, with young people far less likely to support the two largest parties. Were more young Canadians to vote, it seems probable that the party system would be even more fragmented than it is at present, further increasing the pressure for some form of proportional representation.

The tendency of young voters to be more supportive of new parties is found in many countries besides Canada. In Norway, young voters are more likely to direct their votes to the relatively new Socialist Left Party rather than to the traditional left-wing choice of the Labor Party. In Ireland, Sinn Fein gets its votes primarily from the young, whereas the traditional parties of Fianna Fail and Fine Gael are more favored by older voters. Japan's longtime ruling party of Liberal Democrats depends greatly on gaining votes from older voters in order to stay in power, whereas the newer parties like the Democratic Party of Japan draw well among younger voters.[92] And in a variety of countries—Germany, Switzerland, France, Ireland, New Zealand, and Canada—the

TABLE 6.8

Recent Differences in Voting Behavior by Age in Various Democracies

	<30	30–44	45–64	65+	DIFFERENCE BETWEEN 65+ AND <30
GREAT BRITAIN 2005 CONSERVATIVES	26	29	29	35	+9
GREAT BRITAIN 2005 LIBERAL DEMOCRATS	32	25	24	23	−9
CANADA 2004 LIBERALS	31	28	39	40	+9
CANADA 2004 CONSERVATIVES	23	35	30	40	+17
CANADA 2004 NEW DEMOCRATS	24	20	15	11	−13
CANADA 2004 BLOC QUEBECOIS	16	11	12	7	−9
CANADA 2004 GREENS	6	5	4	1	−5
JAPAN 2003 LDP	25	36	38	52	+27
JAPAN 2003 DEMOCRATIC PARTY	36	44	44	28	−8
JAPAN 2003 NEW KOMEITO	27	14	11	14	−13
SWITZERLAND 2003 RADICAL DEMOCRATS	12	11	16	20	+8
SWITZERLAND 2003 SOCIAL DEMOCRATS	27	37	32	21	−6
SWITZERLAND 2003 PEOPLE'S PARTY	18	19	23	29	+11
SWITZERLAND 2003 GREENS	16	8	6	2	−14
GERMANY 2002 CDU/CSU	32	33	31	39	+6
GERMANY 2002 GREENS	17	14	12	8	−9
FRANCE 2002 CHIRAC (RPR)	24	17	18	42	+18
FRANCE 2002 MAMERE (GREENS)	14	10	5	0	−14
NEW ZEALAND 2002 LABOUR	35	41	42	52	+17
NEW ZEALAND 2002 NZ FIRST	2	8	10	14	+12

(Continued)

TABLE 6.8 (Continued)

	<30	30–44	45–64	65+	DIFFERENCE BETWEEN 65+ AND <30
NEW ZEALAND 2002 ACT NZ	9	6	10	3	−6
NEW ZEALAND 2002 GREENS	17	12	5	3	−14
IRELAND 2002 FIANNA FAIL	35	46	51	49	+14
IRELAND 2002 FINE GAEL	17	17	21	26	+9
IRELAND 2002 GREENS	8	6	3	1	−7
IRELAND 2002 SINN FEIN	11	8	3	2	−9
NORWAY 2001 SOCIALIST LEFT	24	16	13	6	−18
NORWAY 2001 LABOR	15	20	25	27	+12
NORWAY 2001 CHRISTIAN PEOPLE'S	10	15	11	19	+9

Source: Comparative Study of Electoral Systems; 2004 Canadian Election Study; 2003 Waseda University Japanese Election Study.

data in Table 6.8 show that the Greens do substantially better with young people than with older voters.

Many of these countries practice some form of proportional representation, thereby giving all parties that exceed a minimal threshold (e.g., at least 5 percent of the national vote) representation in parliament roughly equal to their vote share. However, the fact that young people are so much less likely to vote in these countries means that support for these new parties is underrepresented at the polls. Who votes does make a difference in many established democracies, shaping the alternatives that are presented to the voters as well as affecting the outcome of elections.

Conclusion: A Government for Older People?

As I wrap up my discussion of low youth turnout with students in my American voting behavior class, I like to read them the following newspaper editorial that I found online not long ago:

When it comes to jobs and other issues as well, the manifestoes of the political parties devote surprisingly little space to policies targeting young people. Instead, their pledges are heavily weighted to the concerns of seniors, with this tendency extending to how the budget should be allocated as well.

Some of the responsibility for this situation lies with the younger generations themselves. The voter turnout rate among young people is abysmally low. In the last election, for example, the turnout rate for those in their early 20s was a mere 35 percent. In contrast, 80 percent of people in their 60s cast ballots. To politicians, it is clear which of these two groups demands closer attention and lip service.

If this situation continues, the bills for the nation's massive fiscal budget deficit and the dawdling progress in pension reform will be passed on to the younger generation. The low turnout rate among young voters may very well be viewed as tacit approval for this course of action by lawmakers. We believe that an increase in the ballots cast by those in their 20s would prompt a shift in the leanings of the nation's politicians.

The first step in this journey can begin with this election. We urge all young people of voting age to get out to the polls and exercise their right of choice with a close eye on the future.[93]

I then ask the students what newspaper they think published this editorial. The answers I get are always the usual suspects, that is, the most prominent U.S. newspapers. So when I tell them that this was published in the *Asahi Shimbun*—Japan's largest newspaper (which has an English-language version)—they tend to take special notice. Seeing such an article in a foreign newspaper helps drive home the point that the problem of low youth turnout is not a uniquely American one. The basic arguments made in this Japanese newspaper editorial could easily be made in a wide variety of established democracies around the world.

It has often been said that politics is about answering the question of "Who gets, what, when, and how?" Based on the results of this book, young adults are not likely to figure prominently in the answer to the "who" part of the question. As the *Asahi Shimbun* editorial points out, a significant aspect of the political bias in favor of the elderly involves the issues that make it onto the political agenda. How to take care of a rapidly aging population is dominating political discussion in many countries, whereas concerns regarding young people who face difficulties in starting careers and families often are shunted aside. As American journalist Jane Eisner writes, the generational differences in turnout explain "why the U.S. is a nation where poverty among the elderly was addressed by Medicare and Social Security decades ago, and poverty among children remains a persistent and shameful reality."[94]

The bias toward older people that results from turnout differences between age groups is certainly not intentional on anyone's part. Yet, that does not make it right. Nor does the fact that everyone gets older eventually make the situation any better.

A democracy should always strive to ensure that the views of all eligible voters are represented. Young adults should find that the government listens to them when they are young, not decades later after their needs and views change. The danger inherent in the developments discussed in this book is that if these trends continue unabated, many established democracies will be heading toward "a government of older people, by older people, and for older people."

CHAPTER 7

What Can Be Done?

What can be done to ensure that voting is for young people just as much as it is for other age groups? There is no shortage of ideas among scholars and political commentators. All of these ideas are certainly well intentioned, and I have no qualms in recommending any of them. But if one really wants to solve the problem, and not just make a dent in it, then only one proven solution exists. In the end, I have to agree with Arend Lijphart, who has persuasively argued that "Compulsory voting is the only institutional mechanism . . . that can assure high turnout virtually by itself."[95] This chapter explains how I arrived at this conclusion, first reviewing the other major proposals and then explaining why compulsory voting appears to be the only proven answer to the problem.

HOW TO IMPROVE TURNOUT RATES WITHOUT COMPULSORY VOTING

When I discuss with my students the topic of low youth turnout, one of the most common suggestions they offer is that society should focus on improving civic education. No doubt this could only help boost turnout. As Niemi and Junn's careful research shows, a school civics curriculum enhances what students know about government and politics.[96] And as this book has shown, the lack of political information among young adults is certainly a major source of the problem. In particular, students could benefit greatly from an educational program that teaches them why politics matters to all citizens, as well as to them personally. Even if everyone were to suddenly vote, we would still want to work on civic education in order to foster better-informed voters. The fact that so many young adults don't vote makes the imperative for increased civic education all the more vital.

Yet it must be kept in mind that a concerted effort to increase civic education will yield results only among those who are fairly receptive to being educated. It could thus further accentuate the socioeconomic bias at the polls that was Lijphart's primary concern when he addressed the problem of unequal political participation. Furthermore, any impact from improved civic education is bound to take a long time before becoming evident. The generations who have already left school without picking up the habit of following politics need to be brought into the political system as well, and even the best civic education programs are unlikely to reach many of these young adults.

Because most of my students are Americans, they naturally tend to mention aspects of U.S. campaigns that could be improved so as to facilitate citizen participation. One item that always comes up is making the process of voter registration easier. Because young Americans must register in order to cast their first ballot, and are then likely to be faced with reregistering due to their high levels of mobility, the barriers posed by American registration laws fall most heavily on them. Therefore, anything that can be done to make registration procedures more user-friendly should theoretically benefit young people more than other age groups. State laws that continue to require citizens to register 30 days prior to an election now seem like a product of twentieth-century record-keeping technology. With twenty-first-century computer technology making it possible to update registration files far more expeditiously than in the past, everyone should be given the maximum opportunity to register to vote.

Although it seems good sense to make registration as easy as possible without inviting fraud, even the best registration procedures are unlikely to solve the problem of low youth turnout. Registration has been made significantly easier in the United States over the last three decades—most notably by the passage of the 1993 Motor Voter Act, which required states to permit people to register when they apply for or renew their driver's licenses. Nevertheless, just 52 percent of 18- to 24-year-olds were registered to vote in 2004 as compared to 59 percent in 1972.[97] The next major step in registration reform would be to provide for election day registration, or a comprehensive voter list compiled by the government. Canada permits election day registration throughout the whole country, but it has seen a substantial age gap in turnout develop nonetheless. The governments of Japan and Switzerland compile comprehensive voter registration lists that could serve as models for any country, but getting their young adults to vote has proven far more difficult than getting them registered in recent years.

If the problem of getting young people to vote stems mostly from lack of exposure to politics, as this book argues, then it is no wonder that the results from registration reform have been disappointing. Removing barriers to voting will not have much of an effect if potential voters are not learning much about campaigns for office. Thomas Patterson focuses his attention in *The Vanishing Voter* on the obstacles to learning imposed by the poor design features of American campaigns.[98] Interestingly, Patterson argues that Americans are *over*exposed to presidential campaigns that seem to go on endlessly, concluding that "Nothing would breathe more life into the campaign than shortening it substantially."[99] However, an examination of the survey data collected for Patterson's project reveals that young adults were the least bothered by the length of the 2000 presidential campaign. Forty-nine percent of respondents under 30 said that they preferred a long campaign because it gave them a better chance to know the candidates, compared to 41 percent among respondents aged 30 to 64, and just 28 percent of senior citizens.[100] If one wants to see how shorter campaigns work in practice, one has only to turn to Britain and Canada. Both countries are noted for practicing short electoral campaigns on the order of four to six weeks; yet, their turnout rates have recently fallen to modern lows due to the poor participation rates of their young adults.

This is not to challenge Patterson's basic argument that American turnout rates could be marginally improved via a variety of good government reforms. A system of regional primaries would give the people of every state a meaningful role in choosing the major party candidates. Eliminating the electoral college would give the parties incentive to mobilize voters in every state rather than focus on just the battleground states. And blocks of free TV time for the major parties on every channel could get information about the issues out to more voters.

My own favorite suggestion for improving American turnout involves a simple change in election timing. With an ordinary act of Congress, the date for federal elections could be moved to a leisure day, thereby giving more people more time during election day to vote. The number-one reason that people who are registered but fail to vote give for not participating is that they were too busy with work or school on election day. This excuse is particularly prevalent among young people.[101] So why not change election day from a Tuesday to a weekend or holiday? It is doubtful that any expert on elections would recommend that Afghanistan and Iraq emulate the American example of voting on a Tuesday; so if we wouldn't recommend Tuesday elections to other countries, why should we continue this practice ourselves? By joining the modern world and voting on a leisure day, it is likely that we would experience some increase in election turnout, especially among young people. Yet this suggestion also falls far short of being a panacea when viewed in comparative perspective. Although countries that vote in the middle of the week such as the United States, Canada, Britain, and Ireland are experiencing low turnout among young people, so are a number of other countries that vote on the weekend such as New Zealand, Norway, Japan, and Switzerland.

Much the same case can be made for proportional representation, which has become part and parcel of a modern electoral system. Few experts today would suggest that a new democracy adopt a single-member district system such as long practiced in Britain, Canada, and the United States. Electoral systems that use some form of proportional representation ensure that votes for all the major parties end up counting, especially those for newer protest parties who tend to draw support primarily from young people. However, New Zealand's experience as the first Anglo-American country to change to proportional representation would seem to indicate that such a switch has no more than a marginally positive impact on turnout.[102]

In sum, all of these proposals are worthy suggestions, but even combined they do not amount to a cure-all for generational disparities in turnout. This conclusion should hardly be surprising in light of the findings of Chapters 1–3 of this book, which demonstrated that recent generations have established modern lows for newspaper reading, TV news watching, and knowledge of public affairs. These new generation gaps in following politics are beyond the ability of any governmental reform to reverse. A government of a free country can hardly mandate that people pay attention to political news.

WANT A SOLUTION? CONSIDER COMPULSORY VOTING

Some democracies do, however, require that adult citizens participate in elections or face a small fine.[103] This practice is commonly known as "compulsory voting," but it should be noted that this term is actually somewhat misleading. The secrecy of modern ballots makes it impossible to tell whether an individual has actually voted as opposed to just turned in a blank ballot. Thus, all that can really be required is that citizens show up for elections, not that they actually vote. But given that almost all people who go to the polls under this requirement do indeed make a choice of whom to vote for, and that "compulsory voting" is the commonly used phrase, it seems reasonable to use it with this caveat.

Compulsory voting laws may seem strange to the American ear, but it is an idea that has been tried in a fair number of other countries. Of the 18 established democracies that have been covered in this book, Belgium and Australia have practiced compulsory voting throughout the post–World War II period. If one broadens the sphere a bit to all advanced industrialized societies, then Greece (a democracy since 1974) and tiny Luxembourg can also be added to the list of countries that presently require election attendance by law. In addition, Italy, Austria, and the Netherlands had compulsory voting laws on the books for at least part of the modern era, though enforcement in each of these countries was always weak. By comparison, among the same set of countries, only France, Finland, and the United States elect a president who plays a major role in governing. Thus, presidential government is actually rarer in wealthy democracies than is the practice of requiring citizens to go to the polls.

The best argument for the adoption of compulsory voting is simply that it works extremely well. As Arend Lijphart writes, "Compulsory voting is a particularly effective method to achieve high turnout," even with low penalties and lax enforcement.[104] In particular, the data displayed in Table 7.1 demonstrate that *compulsory voting laws get all age groups out to vote in very high numbers.* The relationship between age and turnout is negligible in all four advanced industrialized countries that currently

TABLE 7.1
Percent Reporting Casting a Ballot by Age in Advanced
Industrialized Countries that Currently have or Recently
had Compulsory Voting Laws

	<30	30–44	45–64	65+	OLDEST/YOUNGEST RATIO
AUSTRIA 2002*	82	90	92	90	1.1 : 1
NETHERLANDS 1998*	88	91	92	94	1.1 : 1
ITALY 2001*	89	92	93	86	1.0 : 1
AUSTRALIA 2004**	97	98	98	99	1.0 : 1
BELGIUM 2004**	89	98	97	92	1.0 : 1
GREECE 2000**	90	93	95	93	1.0 : 1
LUXEMBOURG 1999**	91	93	95	86[v]	.9 : 1

*Recently had a compulsory voting law, but it is no longer in effect.
**Compulsory voting in effect.

[v]Voting is voluntary for citizens aged 70 and over in Luxembourg.

Note: Age is as of the election (not the survey) for Luxembourg, Greece, Italy, and Austria.

Sources: Netherlands, Australia, Belgium: Comparative Study of Electoral Systems; Luxembourg, Greece, Italy, Austria: European Social Survey 2002/3.

practice compulsory voting. Unlike many other democracies that are suffering from abysmally low youth turnout, these four countries have recently experienced turnout rates ranging from 89 to 97 percent among citizens aged 18 to 29.

Furthermore, the impact of compulsory voting laws seems to leave a participatory imprint on societies that continues to be felt even after this practice lapses. Austria, Italy, and the Netherlands no longer require their citizens to vote, but the fact that they formerly did has probably contributed to their continued very high participation rates. Even young people in these countries are voting at high rates, as shown in Table 7.1, perhaps because they have grown up in a country where the government made turnout a high priority at some point and actually required citizen participation.

How Much Support Is There for Compulsory Voting?

One of the most common arguments against the adoption of compulsory voting is that the public just won't stand for it in countries where it is not already in place. How much truth is there to such an assertion? And how much support is there for compulsory voting in countries such as Australia, Belgium, Greece, and Luxembourg where it is being successfully practiced at the present time? The answers are difficult to ascertain given that no cross-national survey has yet asked a question about compulsory voting. However, some country-specific data are available for Australia, Great Britain, Canada, and the United States, which are displayed in Table 7.2.

The survey data from Australia demonstrate that compulsory voting has proven to be a widely popular policy there. Seventy-four percent of respondents to the 2004 Australian Election Study thought that voting at federal elections should be required, and of these people about two out of three said they strongly favored compulsory voting. Such high levels of support have consistently been the case in Australia, with support never falling below 60 percent in data compiled by Mackerras and McAllister dating back to 1943.[105] Interestingly, even young Australians clearly favored compulsory voting in 2004. At the same time, these young respondents were also the least likely to say that they definitely

TABLE 7.2

Support for Compulsory Voting in Australia, Canada, the UK, and the USA by Age (in percents)

	18–29	30–44	45–64	65+	ALL
SUPPORT COMPULSORY VOTING					
AUSTRALIA	75	76	75	74	75
GREAT BRITAIN	37	47	48	56	47
CANADA	40	46	43	58	45
USA	—	—	—	—	21
STRONGLY SUPPORT COMPULSORY VOTING					
AUSTRALIA	39	49	47	50	47
GREAT BRITAIN	20	24	32	42	29
CANADA	15	20	19	34	20

Question wording: Australia—"Do you think that voting at Federal elections should be compulsory, or do you think that people should only have to vote if they want to?" Canada—"In Australia, Belgium, Brazil, and a number of other countries, people are required by law to vote. How supportive would you be of a law like this for federal elections? Would you be very supportive, somewhat supportive, somewhat opposed, or very opposed?" Great Britain—"Which of these policies do you support or oppose? Make voting in elections compulsory." USA—"In a few countries every eligible citizen is required by law to vote in national elections. Those who don't have a good excuse for not voting are subject to a small fine. Do you think this would be a good law or a poor law to have in this country?"

Sources: 2004 Australian Election Study; 2001 MORI survey of Great Britain for the UK Electoral Commission; Elections Canada 2002 survey of voters and nonvoters; June 2004 ABC News survey of USA http://abcnews.go.com/images/pdf/883a44CompulsoryVoting.pdf (accessed August 11, 2005).

would have voted had participation been voluntary.[106] Were it not for mandatory voting, there would be a significant age gap in electoral participation in Australia similar to that found in many other countries. The widespread support for compulsory voting among young Australians indicates that they would rather not see their country slip into this pattern.

Whenever I talk to political science classes in Australia, I find that many Aussie students are amazed to learn how low turnout is for American elections. They immediately ask me why the United States doesn't just emulate their country's example and fine people who fail to participate. The best response I can think of is simply that most Americans object to the government telling them to do something, even if it is good for them. American political culture is based on John Locke's views of individual rights, which differ from Jeremy Bentham's concept of the greatest good for the greatest number, which shaped Australian culture. Most Americans would probably assert that they have an inviolable right not to show up at the polls. As former U.S. Attorney General Griffin Bell remarked during a brief discussion of compulsory voting at a 2001 hearing of the National Commission on Federal Election Reform, "That is not a free country when you are doing things like that."[107] While Griffin Bell's comment may be an extreme reaction, it is apparent from Table 7.2 that there is currently not much support for requiring people to vote in the United States. Only 21 percent of Americans interviewed in a 2004 *ABC News* poll supported the idea of a compulsory voting law like that practiced in Australia.

As Table 7.2 shows, attitudes toward compulsory voting in Canada and Great Britain fall in between the strong support for compulsory voting in Australia and the clear hostility to the idea in the United States. In both countries it is noteworthy that support for compulsory voting increases with age. Among senior citizens in Canada and Great Britain, a majority actually support making voting mandatory. The high level of support for compulsory voting among older citizens can be explained by the facts that voters are substantially more likely than nonvoters to favor it and of course that older people have the highest turnout rate.

Citizens who vote apparently do not want to monopolize political power. Roughly half of voters in both Britain and Canada support the notion that participation by everyone is so important that the government should require it. If politicians listen primarily to those who vote, then they may well start to consider compulsory voting if turnout rates continue to fall, especially among young people. Indeed, a serious rumbling in this direction could be seen after the low turnout in the British general election of 2005. The leader of the British House of Commons, Geoff Hoon, publicly stated that he thought a move to compulsory voting was necessary to reinvigorate UK democracy, arguing that "we need to get people more engaged in political processes."[108]

Is Talk of Compulsory Voting at All Realistic?

When Arend Lijphart called for compulsory voting in his presidential address to the American Political Science Association, he wrote that "The danger of too much pessimism about the chances for compulsory voting is that it becomes a self-fulfilling prophecy. If even the supporters of compulsory voting believe that its chances are nil—and hence make no effort on behalf of it—it will indeed never be adopted!"[109] I wholeheartedly agree. Political scientists have been far too cautious in recommending compulsory voting despite what we know about the seriousness of the turnout problem among young people and how well this solution works to correct it.

Engineering safety experts have not backed off their recommendations calling for mandatory seat belt laws for motorists just because many people think that whether to buckle up or not should be a matter of personal choice. Nor have researchers on secondhand smoke backed off on recommendations to ban smoking in public places just because many people think that such restrictions would be a violation of their individual rights. Rather, these researchers have continued to try to educate people and shift public policy, with the result being a fair degree of success. For example, in 2005 Gallup reported that for the first time, a majority of the American public supported banning smoking in restaurants, up from a mere 17 percent in 1987.[110] As attitudes have changed, so have laws, with 11 U.S. states currently banning smoking in restaurants, and the likelihood is that more will follow suit. The campaign to increase use of safety belts in automobiles has been equally impressive. Every state except New Hampshire now has a law requiring the use of seat belts.[111] Data compiled by the National Highway Traffic Safety Administration on actual usage of seat belts finds that between 1994 and 2005, the percentage of passengers using seat belts increased from 58 to 82 percent.[112] In sum, attitudes and behavior can change as people become more aware of a problem; and once such changes are put into motion, politicians feel compelled to take actions that they never would have even considered a decade earlier.

Ironically, one of the obstacles to the adoption of compulsory voting is the fear of success. Some analysts have trepidations about forcing people with limited political interest to appear at the polls. Once compelled to vote, these citizens may make choices the same way some people choose lottery numbers. Or worse yet, they may be particularly susceptible to demagogic appeals by irresponsible politicians with antidemocratic tendencies. Granted, these are serious concerns. But which is the worse scenario—a low and biased turnout with the participation of only those who follow politics, or a broad and representative turnout with the participation of people who follow politics as well as those who do not? Consider the situation in Italy as of 1959, when the Civic Culture Study found that about two-thirds of Italians said they *never* followed accounts of political and governmental affairs. Italy then had a compulsory voting law, and though it was not rigorously enforced, turnout nevertheless ranged between 92 and 95 percent. Looking back, can one really make a case that it would have been better if only the one-third of the Italian population who followed politics had voted?[113]

In his recent book *Culture War?*, Morris Fiorina writes that his students express outrage at the prospect of being forced to go to the polls even if they don't like any of the candidates.[114] My students, who are of course heavily exposed to the findings reviewed in this book, tend to be more outraged at the fact that older people are running the government while their generation is ignored due to its low turnout rate. The answer to the question posed by the title of this book—*Is Voting for Young People?*—is that it certainly *should* be but all too often is not.

Endnotes

[1] Lara Jakes Jordan, "Harvard Rips Store's 'Old Voter' T-Shirt." Associated Press, March 1, 2004.

[2] See Doris Graber, *Mass Media and American Politics*, 6th ed. (Washington, DC: Congressional Quarterly Press, 2002).

[3] Colleen A. Sheehan, "Madison v. Hamilton: The Battle Over Republicanism and the Role of Public Opinion," *American Political Science Review* 98 (2004): p. 421.

[4] See the September 23, 2003, interview transcript at http://www.foxnews.com/story/0,2933,98111,00.html (accessed February 7, 2004).

[5] See Helen Thomas, "No Wonder Bush Doesn't Connect With the Rest of the Country," Hearst Newspapers, October 15, 2003. See http://seattlepi.nwsource.com/opinion/143851_thomas15.html (accessed February 7, 2004).

[6] *Statistical Abstract of the United States*, 2002, p. 700.

[7] See Philip Meyer, *The Vanishing Newspaper: Saving Journalism in the Information Age* (Columbia, MO: University of Missouri Press, 2004). Also see Frank Ahrens, "Hard News: Daily Papers Face Unprecedented Competition," *Washington Post*, February 20, 2005, p. F1.

[8] Cathy Scott-Clark and Adrian Levy, "Fast Forward Into Trouble," *The Guardian*, June 14, 2003.

[9] The justification for using this definition of regular newspaper reading is that the response options were judgment calls rather than specifics such as "every day." In my view, the major difference is between those who said "often" and "sometimes"—those who basically follow politics through a paper—and those who said "seldom" and "never," those who basically do not. One person's sense of "often" might mean roughly half

the time, while another person's sense of "sometimes" could be exactly the same. But it is hard to see how "seldom" could mean much more than once a week.

[10] Furthermore, the correlations found in the recent European data are probably underestimates because the variance in newspaper reading is truncated due to the poor choice of response categories offered. Most people who responded that they read a newspaper said they read it for less than 30 minutes. When asked the follow-up question of reading about politics, they had little choice but to say they read about politics for less than 30 minutes. There is no doubt a good deal of variation within this category, probably with younger readers spending less time with the newspaper than older ones, but the question's wording does not allow for this variance to be captured.

[11] The correlation between age and having read a book during the past year was −.11 in 1957 and −.04 in 2002. Controlling for education resulted in a partial correlation of −.04 in 1957 and .00 in 2002.

[12] John F. Kennedy, "A Force that Has Changed the Political Scene," *TV Guide*, November 14, 1959. This article can be found online at http://www.museum.tv/debateweb/html/equalizer/tvguide_jfkforce.htm (accessed January 7, 2005).

[13] Thomas E. Patterson and Robert D. McClure, *The Unseeing Eye: The Myth of Television Power in National Elections* (New York: Putnam, 1976), p. 58.

[14] See Paul F. Lazarsfeld et al., *The People's Choice* (New York: Columbia University Press, 1944).

[15] Shanto Iyengar and Donald R. Kinder, *News that Matters* (Chicago: University of Chicago Press, 1987).

[16] Ibid., pp. 118–119.

[17] Joanne M. Miller and Jon A. Krosnick, "News Media Impact on the Ingredients of Presidential Evaluations: Politically Knowledgeable Citizens Are Guided by a Trusted Source," *American Journal of Political Science* (April 2000): pp. 301–315.

[18] Jeff Alan, *Anchoring America: The Changing Face of Network News* (Chicago: Bonus Books, 2003), p. xiii.

[19] Barbara Matusow, *The Evening Stars: The Making of the Network News Anchor* (Boston: Houghton Mifflin, 1983), p. 1.

[20] Frank Rich, "The Weight of an Anchor," *New York Times*, May 19, 2002.

[21] The figure on the average age of the TV news audience can be found in "A Graying, Ailing Audience," *New York Times*, February 9, 2004, p. C6. The figure for a typical prime-time show is cited in Robert D. Putnam, *Bowling Alone: The Collapse and Revival of American Community* (New York: Simon and Schuster, 2000), p. 221.

[22] Pew Research Center for the People and the Press, "Cable and Internet Loom Large in Fragmented Political News Universe." Report released January 11, 2004, p. 10. This report can be found online at http://people-press.org/reports/pdf/200.pdf (accessed January 10, 2005).

[23] Ibid., p. 14.

[24] William Taubman and Jane Taubman, *Moscow Spring* (New York: Summit Books, 1989), p. 286.

[25] Project for Excellence in Journalism, *The State of the News Media, 2004*, posted at http://www.stateofthenewsmedia.org/index.asp (accessed August 27, 2004).

[26] Thomas Rosenstiel, "The End of Network News," *Washington Post*, September 12, 2004, p. B7.

[27] All responses of over 100 were recoded to 100. The correlation between age and the number of channels watched was −.19.

[28] Byron E. Shafer, *Bifurcated Politics: Evolution and Reform in the National Party Convention* (Cambridge, MA: Harvard University Press, 1988), p. 274.

[29] Alan Schroeder, "There's No Debate About It: Face-to-Face, Candidates Let Their Masks Slip," *Washington Post*, October 17, 2004, p. B1. For a good history of these televised encounters, see Schroeder's book, *Presidential Debates: Forty Years of High-Risk TV* (New York: Columbia University Press, 2000).

[30] In 2004, the average presidential debate rating was 33, reflecting the greater interest in this campaign.

[31] Marshall McLuhan, *Understanding Media* (New York: McGraw-Hill, 1964).

[32] Edward J. Epstein, *News from Nowhere: Television and the News* (New York: Random House, 1973).

[33] Ibid., p. 17.

[34] The sample frame included all people at least 16 years of age. The age question did not ask for each respondent's exact age, but rather for an age range. Because the first category was 16 to 20 years of age, one has to either exclude 18-, 19-, and 20-year-olds or include the 16- and 17-year-olds. I

thought it better to include some respondents who were not quite of voting age rather than excluding some respondents who could vote.

[35] The R squared value, measuring the degree to which one variable explains variance in another, increased from .012 in 1970 to .064 in 2000.

[36] An analysis of European Social Survey data from 2002–2003 adds further confidence to this estimate. This survey asked Europeans, "On an average weekday, how much time, in total, do you spend watching television? And again on an average weekday, how much of your time watching television is spent watching *news* or programmes about *politics and current affairs?*" The average correlation between age and the number of minutes spent watching news about politics was .29 in the 12 established democracies other than Italy (which once again was found to be an outlying case).

[37] In spite of winning these debates, both John Turner in Canada and Mark Latham in Australia saw their respective parties lose the election. As John Kerry found out in the United States, success in televised debates is no guarantee of victory at the polls.

[38] Australian Associated Press, "Australian Idol Beats Election Debate," September 13, 2004.

[39] James T. Hamilton, *All the News That's Fit to Sell* (Princeton: Princeton University Press, 2004), p. 7.

[40] Ibid., p. 70.

[41] Matthew A. Baum, *Soft News Goes to War: Public Opinion and American Foreign Policy in the New Media Age* (Princeton: Princeton University Press, 2003), p. 7.

[42] David T. Z. Mindich, *Tuned Out: Why Americans Under 40 Don't Follow the News* (New York: Oxford University Press, 2005), p. 39.

[43] Ibid., p. 40.

[44] See Norman Nie, Jane Junn, and Kenneth Stehlik-Barry, *Education and Democratic Citizenship in America* (Chicago: University of Chicago Press, 1996), pp. 114–118.

[45] See Michael X. Delli Carpini and Scott Keeter, *What Americans Know About Politics and Why It Matters* (New Haven, CT: Yale University Press, 1996), pp. 196–199. In their detailed analysis over time, Delli Carpini and Keeter also conclude that the relative impact of education on political knowledge has been fairly constant over the past half century.

[46] Gabriel A. Almond and Sidney Verba, *The Civic Culture* (Boston: Little, Brown, and Co., 1963), pp. 206–207.

[47] Ibid., p. 308.

[48] Ibid., p. 57.

[49] I initially created two separate indices—one for the number of Common Market countries named, and the other for recall of the two political leaders. The results by age were almost identical for these two indices, and therefore I have combined them to simplify the presentation.

[50] The data on who won *American Idol* and the TV Simpsons' hometown can be found in Karl T. Kurtz, Alan Rosenthal, and Cliff Zukin, "Citizenship: A Challenge for All Generations." Report of the National Conference of State Legislatures, September 2003. This report can be found at http://www.cpn.org/topics/youth/k12/pdfs/NCSL_Citizenship.pdf (accessed March 4, 2005). The data on the Super Bowl winner is from Harvard's 2000 "Vanishing Voter" project.

[51] Stephen Earl Bennett and Eric W. Rademacher, "The Age of Indifference Revisited: Patterns of Political Interest, Media Exposure, and Knowledge among Generation X," in *After the Boom: The Politics of Generation X*, ed. Stephen C. Craig and Stephen Earl Bennett, p. 39 (Lanham, MD: Rowman and Littlefield, 1997).

[52] Michael X. Delli Carpini and Scott Keeter, *What Americans Know About Politics and Why It Matters* (New Haven, CT: Yale University Press, 1996), chap. 6.

[53] Of course, political scientists have come up with many reasons for why people vote. For a review of the factors that influence who votes, see Raymond E. Wolfinger and Steven J. Rosenstone, *Who Votes?* (New Haven, CT: Yale University Press, 1980) and Martin P. Wattenberg, *Where Have All the Voters Gone?* (Cambridge, MA: Harvard University Press, 2002), chap. 3.

[54] See U.S. Bureau of the Census, *Current Population Reports*, Series P-20, No. 143, "Voter Participation in the National Election: November 1964." Washington, DC: U.S. Government Printing Office, 1965, p. 1. This report can be found at http://www.census.gov/population/www/socdemo/voting/p20-143.html (accessed June 11, 2005).

[55] President's Commission on Registration and Voting Participation, "Report on Registration and Voting Participation." Washington, DC: U.S. Government Printing Office, 1963, p. 43.

[56] Jane Eisner, *Taking Back the Vote: Getting American Youth Involved in Our Democracy* (Boston: Beacon Press, 2004), p. 3.

[57] Alexander Keyssar, *The Right to Vote: The Contested History of Democracy in the United States* (New York: Basic Books, 2000), p. 281.

[58] Quoted in Eisner, *Taking Back the Vote*, p. 31.

[59] Benjamin Highton and Raymond E. Wolfinger, "The First Seven Years of the Political Life Cycle," *American Journal of Political Science* 45 (2001): pp. 202–209.

[60] The information for these age categories can be found at http://www.census.gov/population/www/socdemo/voting.html (accessed June 21, 2005).

[61] Following the framework outlined in Russell J. Dalton and Martin P. Wattenberg, eds., *Parties Without Partisans* (Oxford: Oxford University Press, 2001), p. 14, I have limited the sample of countries to those that: 1) have been democracies continuously since World War II; 2) belong to the OECD; and 3) have substantial population size (thereby excluding Iceland and Luxembourg).

Whenever possible, I have used data from national election studies, choosing the time point closest to November 1972. For countries that had no election studies available—Finland, Austria, and Italy—I used data from the Political Action Study that asked respondents whether they had voted in the most recent national election.

[62] On this question in Denmark, see Jorgen Elklit, Palle Svensson, and Lise Togeby, "Why Is Voter Turnout Not Declining in Denmark?" Paper presented at the 2005 meeting of the American Political Science Association.

[63] Mark N. Franklin, *Voter Turnout and the Dynamics of Electoral Competition in Established Democracies Since 1945* (New York: Cambridge University Press, 2004), p. 206.

[64] The legal specification is actually more complex. The National Voter Registration Act of 1993 states that removal can occur only if someone "has not voted or appeared to vote (and, if necessary, correct the registrar's record of the registrant's address) in an election during the period beginning on the date of the notice and ending on the day after the date of the second general election for Federal office that occurs after the date of the notice." In practice, this amounts to roughly four years before someone can be purged.

[65] Alan Ware, *The Breakdown of Democratic Party Organization, 1940–1980* (New York: Oxford, 1985), p. 203.

[66] I am indebted to Mark Gray for obtaining and processing these data and making them available to me.

[67] Voting in local government elections is compulsory in some Australian states, and it is interesting to note the differences in voter turnout rates in such elections. In New South Wales and Queensland, for example, where voting is compulsory, turnout rates were more than 85 percent in recent elections. But in other states, where voting in local government elections is not compulsory, turnout rates were much lower. For example, only about 58 percent of enrolled people voted in Tasmania's 2002 local election, and only 38 percent voted in Western Australia's May 2001 local election.

[68] In 2001 the Western Australian Electoral Commission found nearly identical results by age.

[69] See the October/November 2002 Eurobarometer. Thirty-six percent said this statement was false, and 21 percent said they did not know.

[70] The turnout figures for each country from 1979 to 2004 can be found at http://www.elections2004.eu.int/ep-election/sites/en/results1306/ turnout_ep/turnout_table.html (accessed July 5, 2005).

[71] Data from the June 2004 European Parliamentary elections have been collected, but they were not yet publicly available at the time of this writing.

[72] Franklin, *Voter Turnout*, p. 213.

[73] Interestingly, Mark Franklin writes favorably about this idea, arguing that this probably would work better than the current voting age of 18 practiced in most countries. See note 72.

[74] In most national surveys, there would not be sufficient cases to do such an analysis with such narrowly defined age groups. The fact that the European Social Survey was conducted in numerous countries makes it possible to aggregate more than enough cases to get a reliable reading on the media habits of 16- to 17-year-olds.

[75] Angus Campbell, Philip E. Converse, Warren E. Miller, and Donald E. Stokes, *The American Voter* (Chicago: University of Chicago Press, 1960), p. 105.

[76] Andre Blais, *To Vote or Not to Vote* (Pittsburgh: University of Pittsburgh Press, 2000), p. 92.

[77] I first went on a scouting trip to see if there was a wheelchair at the polling place, without which I figured it would be next to impossible for my father to vote. There indeed was one, but I noticed there was a lot of competition for access to it. When I reported back to my parents that they might have to

wait a while for my father to get use of the wheelchair, they said this was all right. We proceeded to the polling place, and all went well. It was while waiting for my parents to vote that I observed that the average age of people voting in this midterm election was quite high, and the idea for this book was first hatched in my own mind.

[78] Two percent picked all, 1 percent said none, and 2 percent said they didn't know.

[79] Blais, *To Vote or Not to Vote*, p. 97.

[80] M. Kent Jennings and Richard G. Niemi, *The Political Character of Adolescence: The Influence of Families and Schools* (Princeton: Princeton University Press, 1974), p. 122.

[81] M. Kent Jennings and Richard G. Niemi, *Generations and Politics: A Panel Study of Young Adults and Their Parents* (Princeton: Princeton University Press, 1981), p. 125.

[82] In 1997, data were also gathered from a sample of the children of the class of 1965. However, as this third-generation sample was contacted only by mail, they were not asked the open-ended question concerning the qualities of a good citizen.

[83] Raymond E. Wolfinger and Steven J. Rosenstone, *Who Votes?* (New Haven, CT: Yale University Press, 1980), p. 111.

[84] Ruy A Teixeira, *The Disappearing American Voter* (Washington, DC: The Brookings Institution, 1992), p. 95.

[85] Sidney Verba, Kay Lehman Schlozman, and Henry E. Brady, *Voice and Equality: Civic Voluntarism in American Politics* (Cambridge, MA: Harvard University Press, 1995), p. 205.

[86] David R. Mayhew, *Congress: The Electoral Connection* (New Haven, CT: Yale University Press, 1974).

[87] John W. Kingdon, *Agendas, Alternatives, and Public Policies*, 2nd ed. (New York: Harper Collins, 1995).

[88] Other data collections, such as the American National Election Studies, the Pew Research Center surveys, and the National Annenberg Election Study, confirm this pattern.

[89] Because nonvoters tend to be less conservative than voters, it is hard to see how they would have voted more for Bush. Thus, making this assumption probably involves slightly underestimating just how much equalizing the turnout rate among ages would have swung the vote in Gore's favor.

[90] See Russell J. Dalton, *Citizen Politics: Public Opinion and Political Parties in Advanced Industrial Democracies*, 3rd ed. (Chatham, NJ: Chatham House, 2002).

[91] Excluding the countries that practice compulsory voting—Australia and Belgium—increases the correlation to .80.

[92] I am indebted to Aiji Tanaka of Waseda University for sharing his 2003 survey data with me for this purpose.

[93] Editorial, *Asahi Shimbun*, November 3, 2003.

[94] Jane Eisner, *Taking Back the Vote: Getting American Youth Involved in Our Democracy* (Boston: Beacon Press, 2004), p. 54.

[95] Arend Lijphart, "Unequal Participation: Democracy's Unresolved Dilemma," *American Political Science Review* 91 (1997): p. 10.

[96] Richard G. Niemi and Jane Junn, *Civic Education: What Makes Students Learn* (New Haven, CT: Yale University Press, 1998).

[97] Among citizens aged 18 to 24, the registration rate in 2004 was 58 percent. Unfortunately, the 1972 Census survey did not ascertain citizenship status. My best guess—based on the relatively small percentage of noncitizens then living in the United States—is that roughly 61 percent of 18- to 24-year-old citizens were registered to vote.

[98] Thomas E. Patterson, *The Vanishing Voter* (New York: Knopf, 2002). See p. 182 for a list of Patterson's policy proposals.

[99] Ibid., p. 149.

[100] The question wording was as follows: "Some people say the presidential campaign is so long that they don't have time to pay attention except now and then. Other people say they like the long presidential campaign because it gives them a better chance to get to know the candidates. Which view is closer to your own? Do you think the campaign is too long or do you prefer a long campaign?" This question was asked in six different weekly surveys, and was answered by a total of 2255 respondents.

[101] In 2002, the U.S. Census Bureau found that 30 percent of registered nonvoters aged 18 to 24 said they were too busy to vote on election day, whereas only 5 percent of senior citizens who were registered and did not vote chose this excuse.

[102] Jack Vowles, "Offsetting the PR Effect? Party Mobilization and Turnout Decline in New Zealand, 1996–99," *Party Politics* 8 (2002): pp. 587–605.

[103] In Australia the typical fine for nonvoting is 20 Australian dollars. However, judges typically accept any reasonable excuse, and few people end up paying a fine for not voting. In the Australian federal election of 2004, there were about 13 million enrolled voters, 94.3 percent of whom participated. Of the approximately 740,000 nonvoters, only about 50,000 actually paid a fine.

[104] Lijphart, "Unequal Participation," p. 2.

[105] Malcolm Mackerras and Ian McAllister, "Compulsory Voting, Party Stability, and Electoral Advantage in Australia," *Electoral Studies* 18 (1999): p. 221.

[106] Fifty-four percent of people between the ages of 18 and 29 said they would definitely have voted in 2004 had voting been voluntary, compared to 77 percent among Australian senior citizens.

[107] Judge Griffin Bell, National Commission on Federal Election Reform, Public Hearing 1, Panel IV, transcript, p. 13.

[108] *BBC News World Edition*, "Hoon Suggests Compulsory Voting," July 4, 2005.

[109] Lijphart, "Unequal Participation," p. 11.

[110] David W. Moore, "Increased Support for Smoking Bans in Public Places," *Gallup Poll Report*, July 20, 2005.

[111] Twenty states have primary-enforcement laws, meaning that motorists can be given a ticket for no reason other than simply not fastening their seat belt. Twenty-nine other states have secondary-enforcement laws, whereby drivers must be stopped for another violation before being given a citation for not using a seat belt.

[112] Donna Glassbrenner, "Safety Belt Use in 2005—Overall Results." Traffic Safety Facts Research Note, August 2005, National Highway Traffic Safety Administration. http://www-nrd.nhtsa.dot.gov/pdf/nrd-30/NCSA/RNotes/2005/809932.pdf (accessed November 5, 2005). In states with primary-enforcement laws, this study found that 85 percent of passengers were buckled up in 2005, compared to 75 percent in states with secondary-enforcement laws.

[113] Lest one think that an established democracy could never see such low turnout for a national election, I'd point out that turnout rates for U.S. midterm congressional elections have regularly been between 33 and 40 percent in recent decades.

[114] Morris P. Fiorina (with Samuel J. Abrams and Jeremy C. Pope), *Culture War?* (New York: Longman, 2005), p. 111.

Name Index

Subject Index